One in a Million

Everything You Need to Know to Find the *Best* Realtor

Erik Brown

First published by Dog Ear Publishing
4011 Vincennes Rd
Indianapolis, IN 46268
www.dogearpublishing.net

ISBN: 978-1-4575-4929-8

This book is printed on acid-free paper.

Printed in the United States of America

Written for those who dream Big.

Contents

Foreword

To borrow the words of Dickens, "It was the best of times, it was the worst of times…" The year was 2009. The real estate community was in the trenches of the worst crisis it had experienced in modern times. It was two years earlier that we started watching the unraveling of the market, as if someone had pulled at a small string on the sleeve of a giant sweater and slowly but surely all we had left was a pile of shapeless yarn. Every real estate agent and broker in the country was surrounded by the devastation. A devastation, I might add, from which we have yet to fully recover.

Though the collapsing house of cards that was the real estate market had a real and huge toll on the American economy and the average American household, it did have some good side effects. The real estate agents and brokers who were simply in the business to make a quick buck and had no real or deep value started dropping like flies. With them went agents and brokers who could not adapt to new technology and ways of doing business. The last group of agents and brokers to fail in this new market reality were the ones that simply did not put their client's interests above their own and who did not deliver the utmost customer service.

In February of 2009, I met Erik Brown. I had recently become the broker of RE/MAX Results in the Twin Cities area of Minnesota. He immediately struck me as someone who would survive and thrive in the shambles of the Great Recession. He had a passion for the business and for his clients, and he adopted new practices and technology not with the resigned sigh of a beaten businessperson, but with the excitement and energy of an innovator. It was clear this guy was going somewhere.

Here's a secret about the book you are about to read. It's not what it claims to be…or at least it's a lot more than it claims to be. It says in the title that it is a guide to how to FIND the right real estate agent. And it is. But this book is also, and I'd say primarily, a guide on how to BE the right real estate agent. Every agent and broker across the country would be well served to read this book and modify their attitudes and methods to conform to its tenets.

It's not good enough to be just a good real estate agent. "Average" is killing our industry. The consumer has come to expect average agents because that is what they get 90 percent of the time. That is why real estate agents rank below politicians and used-car sales-people in the lists of "who do you trust." Stop giving your business to good real estate agents. Start trusting and relying upon GREAT real estate agents. They're out there. You just have to look and find them. Erik is one of those agents and he has written this book to help you find them.

Many industries have the 80/20 rule, where 80 percent of the business is produced by 20 percent of the participants. I think in real estate it might be closer to the 90/10 rule, or maybe even the 95/5 rule. I'm telling you, there is a difference in the agent you choose. Marketing and negotiation are skills honed through education and experience. Any agent can throw your listing on the MLS, but can they truly assess the market to list at the right price, market it properly, and then navigate an offer and negotiate it to the breaking point without going past it?

So I ask you, no, I plead with you. Stop using just good real estate agents. Seek the very best in the industry. Then, slowly, all of the simply good (and worse) real estate agents will leave the business. The real estate agent will rise in the estimation of the consumer and we will all benefit. Use this book as your guide.

—*Marshall Saunders*
Founder, Saunders Daily

Introduction:

The Negotiator

In Denver, real estate agent Tim often shared that it was his duty to get his home seller clients the best deal possible. That's why he was shocked when another agent called him to let him know there were buyers interested in his listing; said agent confided in Tim that they would be willing to pay the full asking price in spite of his buyer client's offer for $25,000 less. "Of course the reason this agent told me this was because he wanted to make sure the offer got accepted so he would get paid. He knew he was backstabbing his clients by putting his own interests above theirs," Tim said. As luck would have it, Tim's listing received a higher offer before the other could go to closing, so the "negotiating" buyer's agent had gained nothing beyond a bad reputation. Sadly, his clients were not the wiser.

Realtor with Benefits

After what they felt to be a thorough search, San Francisco home-owners Kathy and Miguel entrusted real estate agent Robert to sell their home. The detail-oriented couple equipped their home with motion-activated cameras, moved out, and waited for Robert to make a deal on their vacant house.

One night, when the cameras turned on in their former home, Kathy called the police. Officers arrived thinking there was a burglary. Instead, they found Robert in the dark house with a woman.

When Kathy and Miguel couldn't understand why their real estate agent was in their home so late and were not given an answer, the couple hit the rewind button on their cameras and discovered shocking video. They found day after day of X-rated videos of Robert and the woman, another agent. Disgusted, the couple sued the agents and their brokerage for damages.

Bait and Switch

Brent was a real estate agent for a seller whose condo had languished for several months, but was thrilled to get a cash offer from a mature woman with disabilities. The buyer included a proof-of-funds letter from an investment brokerage firm, asked many thoughtful and articulate questions, and was prompt in signing documents. It was like a dream come true for the seller. At the closing, as the title company closing agent finalized all the paperwork, they mentioned that the buyer's funds had not been wired yet. As they waited, Brent passed the keys off to the buyer and the buyer's agent. Minutes passed. The buyer and agent said they would contact the bank and make sure the transfer was completed, and then left. Since the title work was finished, Brent assumed all was fine...until he received a call from his brokerage that the earnest deposit check bounced and the proof-of-funds letter had a forged signature. The would-be buyer and agent vanished, but not before attempting to take items from the home with their newfound keys.

Are these stories extreme? Maybe, but agent issues can and do happen every day. Bizarre, but these are three stories I have heard, witnessed, or read about (with names and locations edited) to show just a few of the marvels of the unprofessional and underprepared real estate agent. When buying or selling a home, there are hundreds of moving parts, and the real estate agent is in charge of the majority of them. In most homes in every town, every week, e-mails, postcards, and knocks on the door arrive touting "service" and "expertise" from an agent interested in assisting you with your real estate goals. The amount of white noise can be deafening, and creating a true apples-to-apples comparison seems impossible. With literally millions of real estate agents in the world, you may wonder if it even matters which one you pick.

I never dreamed of working in real estate. I had watched *The Money Pit*, a 1980s flick about a dilapidated house and its unsuspecting buyers, but that was the extent of my property interests.

From my earliest years, I was going to be an astronaut, fireman, artist, lawyer, and finally, a professional basketball player. It's not like I was a dreamer; I was a typical kid who didn't know what I wanted to be when I grew up. Even so, I did have an inherent knack for sales and hustle. I used to pool-shark other kids in my neighborhood for baseball cards by pretending to be terrible at billiards before winning their Ken Griffey Jr. rookie cards. I traded a GI Joe helicopter for a full set of Garbage Pail Kids because I thought they would have more collector value. At twelve, a friend and I convinced our local Hardee's restaurant that we were of working age so we could dress up as Burger Bear and wave to other kids for $2.50 per hour. I liked to earn a buck, but at no point in my formative years did I imagine being self-employed or working in any capacity of sales, advising, or realty.

The seeds of change were planted the summer before my junior year in college. For the love of all things athletic, I wanted to have a career in some capacity in the National Basketball Association. Recognizing that my actual game skills were more Hickory High than His Airness, I sweet-talked my way into the ticket sales office of the Minnesota Timberwolves, spending weeks of my free time stuffing envelopes, grabbing coffees, stapling and collating anything and everything I could to prove my worth. The effort paid off—when the team announced a summer work program, I beat out over a thousand applicants to become what felt like NBA royalty: head intern of community basketball relations. True, this may not have been CEO of a Fortune 500 company, but I did have a custom name tag; six of one, half dozen of the other. Over the next several months, I assisted in the management of summer basketball camps. Each camp not only taught the fundamentals of basketball, but also the foundational stepping-stones of being a good teammate and better person. Witnessing and facilitating this youth development was inspiring.

As I rounded out my final year of school in the late 90s, the economy was booming, and "consulting" as a career choice was all the rage. Business firms were giving away jobs like candy at a parade, and the salaries offered for an eager twenty-two-year-old made me salivate at the thought of paying off school debt within my lifetime. After graduation and staring in the face of an NBA labor lockout, I chose financial freedom over professional sports and began a career as a consultant, traveling to such exotic locales as Cleveland, Indianapolis, and Dearborn, Michigan, teaching the miracles of enterprise resource planning and software upgrades. Bouncing from city to city, a few colleagues and I would pass time in the cabs, shuttle buses, and airports by reading various money-making books and get-rich-quick schemes. Yes, I still liked the hustle. On one such shuttle ride, youthful enthusiasm boiled over as we expounded on yet another wild-haired idea to build a business empire. As we blustered back and forth, I noticed a well-groomed middle-aged man passively listening to us carry on about making millions. Laid-back and exuding success, he seemed to be amused by our ideological rants. I paid no mind until, after several minutes of listening to us exclaim in wild-eyed fashion all the ways we would theoretically develop our wealth, he leaned in and offered a suggestion. "Fellas," he said, "Your books sound fascinating. Have you thought about reading something with a bit more...substance?"

We sat, somewhat stupefied, not knowing really what he meant by the question. Over the next several minutes, the curious stranger introduced himself as the owner of a multi-location regional business, and shared insights, concepts, and philosophies that had never, not once, crossed our inexperienced minds. He mentioned that we reminded him of himself at a young age, and as we sat wide-eyed and engaged, he proceeded to share a few book titles, professional contacts, and ideas we should consider. The cherry was dropped atop the sundae he shared when he asked us, "Why?" Why do you want to do these things? What is your purpose? It was like being downloaded into *The Matrix* for a few minutes. We had no idea. Just as fast as he connected with us, he wished us luck and stepped off the bus at the next stop. It was all a blur, a blink, but a lasting lesson that piqued my entrepreneurial curiosity and sense of greater purpose. Wherever you are, Dallas traveler and business-man circa 1999, thank you.

Unbeknownst to me at the time, that random conversation was one of several awakenings that kept pushing me toward self-employment and the development of something outside my com-fort zone. I loved the idea of chasing passions while giving back to the greater good, to society as a whole. So I took the plunge. Later that year, one year removed from college, I began a path that over the next seventeen years saw me buy, fix, and sell dozens of homes, get a general contractor's license, start and sell a property manage-ment company, start and crash a boutique title insurance company, and build a real estate team from scratch, in two different states, simultaneously.

We are all a product of our experiences, and from that day in Texas, I turned into a sponge for all things real estate. I have read dozens of books, met hundreds of successful agents, attended realty and investment classes and international conferences, and paid for and learned from dozens of well-respected realty and business coaches. I've had the good fortune to work with many successful brokers and peers that created wildly effective and well-respected busi-nesses before me, and who shared the gift of their knowledge and experience. I share this because I believe in paying it forward, in karma, in building trusting relationships more than building trans-actions.

For most, selling or buying a home will be one of, if not *the* largest, financial decisions a person can make. I want to make sure the people you surround yourself with are going to be at the top of their game for you. Better yet, I want you to meet professionals who will enhance not just you and your experience, but the industry as a whole and the greater good.

In today's age of 24/7 media coverage, TV personalities, and mass marketing, it seems you can throw a rock in any direction and hit a Realtor. It can be difficult to separate the wheat from the chaff. In addition, we are in the middle of a demographic earthquake that rumbles louder each day; Baby Boomers, Millennials, household changes, and global changes. These tremors in our housing make-up create trials and complexities for the profession not experienced before, meaning the professionals charged with helping you on one of the largest purchases or sales of your life had better be at the top of their game. I looked at the challenge of the market, the industry, and the cast of characters that make it up, and asked a simple question: "What is the difference between a good agent and a bad or mediocre one?"

This book is broken into three main topics:

1. Why are there good and bad agents?
2. How do you see the difference?
3. What characteristics define an extraordinary one?

Many of the things I suggest are just common sense. In fact, the main difference between a great Realtor and a bad one can be summed up in a few sentences. I could probably text you quick answers faster than you could read the back cover of this book, but I'd bet a shiny quarter that the message to be shared would lose most of its luster. It would lack impact, and you wouldn't get much out of it. Besides, you'll find many stellar examples of differentiation inside these pages, examples that you can apply. To excel at anything, you have to take massive action, and this book allows you to do so on the grand stage of home buying and selling.

At the end of most chapters, you will find a Last Word section, a tip that summarizes the ideas of the section. This is the gold nugget, the 3 x 5 card that gives you the highlights version of the meatier details that preceded it.

There is a bonus beyond "just" knowing the difference between good and bad real estate professionals. After this read, you'll have the knowledge to find someone who can help you make or save tens or hundreds of thousands of dollars over your lifetime. Read that again. Tens or hundreds of thousands of dollars. Skeptical? From costs saved to investment opportunities, follow these pages and read the tips shared. You'll have the tools to find a professional who will help you achieve and exceed all your real estate goals, goals that can apply to other aspects of your personal and business worlds.

All that said, I'm going to throw down the gauntlet and offer a challenge. If you told me you wanted to learn another language and I suggested you might buy a Rosetta Stone CD or join a language club, would you do it? Would you take the basic steps to succeed? You can bring a horse to water, but you can't make him drink. My challenge, now that you have picked up this book and shown even an iota of real estate interest, is to find all the hidden gems in these pages that can guide you to all levels of real estate successes. I have A LOT more to share with you, and I don't think it will take you long to see how much more you can gain from me than can fit in these pages. In fact, I've got several free offers at the end of this book I want you to take advantage of. To take the next step is risk and cost free. I encourage you not to skip ahead, but instead soak up the knowledge in these pages prior to getting your free gifts. You'll then have a basis for what you can receive.

I am giving away the secrets of years of applied knowledge and practical application in these pages because so much of what I do is based on delivering value to my clients and the people in my life. If this helps the competition improve, it also helps the industry and all homeowners and home buyers. I can't help every home seller and buyer directly, but I can give back through these chapters. This book may teach you something new, but just as importantly, it is a systematic approach that will help you apply what you learn to greater good for you and those you care about. Enjoy the read.

BOOK 1

What is the Problem?

CHAPTER 1

Setting the Stage

*"The difference between genius and stupidity
is that genius has its limits."*
—Albert Einstein

I n the documentary *The Inside Job*, Matt Damon narrates the global financial meltdown of 2008 that caused millions of job and home losses and plunged the United States into a deep economic recession. The film shares the key elements that led to the collapse and identifies the financial and political players that were instrumental in an economic fall that had wide-reaching effects. From the United States to China, Iceland, and beyond, the world took notice of the United States' largest economic crisis since the Great Depression.

What the $%&@# happened? The American financial industry had been regulated from the dawn of WWII to the early 1980s. As comfort in the American financial system grew, bankers and investors wanted to increase returns by deregulating the finance industry; in essence, to make conservative investments less secure, but also increasing possible returns. High risk, high reward. Over the next several decades, investments like savings and loans in the 80s, derivatives in the 90s, and Internet stocks in the 2000s added to our overall economic instability. Banks grew in power and flexibility. Cue the beginning horror music as Jaws enters the waters of Amity, Maine.

At the time, the financial industry was dominated by investment banks like Goldman Sachs and Lehman Brothers, insurance companies like AIG, and rating agencies like Moody's and Standard & Poor's. Investment banks bundled mortgages with other loans and debts, which they sold to investors. The rating agencies gave many of these bundles fantastic ratings, creating a market for riskier loan products for consumers. Buh…bum. Buh…bum. Bum bum bum bum… As more and more people wanted to own a home, banks and mortgage companies created less stringent qualifications to help them purchase, causing a heightened destabilization of the housing industry. These subprime loans led to predatory lending, and many homeowners were given loans they could never repay.

Over the next several years, thousands of homeowners began to default on their loans, leaving banks and financial institutions holding the bag. The federal government stepped in, offering hundreds of billions in bailout money to the institutions. The global financial system became paralyzed. Job layoffs and home foreclosures escalated, with unemployment rising to 10 percent in the United States and the European Union. The financial "sheet" finally hit the fan.

Any market has highs and lows, from stocks to commodities, and the same can be said for the real estate industry. Before the wheel of economic recovery began to spin, the profession had already lost hundreds of thousands of agents. When opportunities dry up, people move to greener pastures. This is not a bad thing. It may sound Darwinian, but in a capitalistic market, there is only survival of the fittest. Ebbs and flows, retraction and expansion. By necessity, this creates a stronger breed of agent, one more prepared to handle the complexities of the industry. Given time and an improving economy, new agent licensees began to increase. An improved housing market brings improved income opportunities, and with it, new service providers. Greener pastures once more.

What is interesting about these highs and lows is that the average age of a real estate agent had been hovering around his or her mid-fifties for decades. Harder barriers to entry, lack of consistent pay, a high learning curve, and unrealistic expectations of the work required are some of the main culprits. With a rollercoaster flow of agents moving in and out of the profession, the gap in talent, experience level, and product knowledge is at an all-time high. With this type of gap, it is easy to see how a home buyer or seller could pick an agent who is the lesser of two evils. As more agents come into the marketplace, competition increases. With new rivals, the reality for most practitioners is one of ill-fated attempts to stand out in a crowd of me toos...all yelling "Choose me, I'm better," blah, blah, blah. When you are interested in working with an agent, maybe you pick someone with a flashy website and a stack of business cards, or an agent with a few neighborhood signs and a healthy amount of confidence to boot. This may seem obvious on paper, but a big self-promotion marketing budget and well-practiced presentation does not equal actual talent or ability.

In a recent Gallup Poll, the question was asked of consumers, "How would you rate the honesty and ethical standards of people in a select group of industries?" Real estate agents ranked in the bottom third of professions listed, barely ahead of car salespeople and telemarketers, and slightly behind lawyers and bankers. Curses! Why such a bad reputation? Sadly, the majority of agents lack the skills to not only help their clients, but foster a culture of honesty. Home buyers and sellers can feel like a tasty paycheck to a hungry agent. Business challenges like this and others make it difficult for many agents to forge a meaningful career. Every year, hundreds of thousands of licensees fail to close a single deal. In some areas, up to 80 percent of new agents fail to renew their license on their first renewal date. Today, the best estimates indicate that 10 percent of the agents are still conducting about 90 percent of the business. Paretto and his 80-20 rule? Please.

Think about what really matters when making decisions about a product or service, and consider what makes a professional's service in any field stand out to you. It can get especially nerve-racking when the decision you make could have dramatic consequences if you get said decision wrong. When making an important choice like buying or selling a home, you are probably looking for a few critical clues to help make informed decisions. It's just a guess, but I bet you probably look for people with real experience. For example, you probably don't want a doctor who got his degree from a medical correspondence school in a third world country; or a stock broker who thinks the best way to make investment decisions is to throw darts at the *Wall Street Journal.*

You know what else is important? Trust. Likeability. As consumers, we select products and services in an environment we enjoy, an environment that makes us feel part of the club. Think Dollar Shave Club for men and the cool factor they bring in their marketing and storytelling. All this for *razors*; their customers love them. It is rare to find one or the other from an unlikeable, untrustworthy business. People don't do business with businesses; we do business with *people*. We invest our time with someone we like, not someone who thinks kindness is for weak-minded people and bathing is optional (sorry, I just assume they stink). I think these things are important to us all, because if we get this decision wrong, especially in real estate, the time, money, and mental and emotional distress could be very costly. One of the biggest judgment calls we make isn't actually when we are choosing to do business with someone. No, the biggest judgment calls we are likely to make are when we are choosing the people we will spend the most time with—friends, coworkers, and spouses. When the product is you or the product is someone else, that is when you are most critical about the decisions you make. If you make the wrong choice, it can be the most painful, most emotional, most expensive, and biggest waste of time in your life.

This same holds true when selecting an agent, because we spend a lot of time with them at a very critical time, making a very large decision. It is important to understand that not every agent does the same things to help buy or sell. As with any job, some are better than others, and some prefer to do the bare minimum as long as they can get away with it. Obviously, these Realtors are not the best choice. To get the best experience, service, systems, the best everything from your professional, you want a real estate agent who is willing to put in the time and effort it takes to prove successful results. There is no magic pill, but there is a formula.

The Constitution says that all men are created equal, but believe me when I tell you this does not apply to agents. Here are a few types of agents you may want to avoid while deciding on your home goals:

The Rookie or Part Timer
In the book *Trump: The Art of the Deal*, Donald Trump tells his key to success in real estate: If you take care of the downside, the upside will take care of itself. In other words, if you have a contingency plan for everything that can go wrong, you can't help but succeed. No matter what you believe about his political convictions, the Donald absolutely has a knack for success.

Real estate is a full-time job and cannot be effectively shared with anything else. Not to beat a dead horse, but would you hire a doctor who only practiced medicine part time? If not guided correctly or creating the time to build the necessary experience, new or part-time agents will have a hard time actively following the market and its changing trends. If you're buying, you want an agent who can jump on new listings and show them to you immediately, break down the good deals, and get you the home. Excuses be damned.

If you're the seller, you want an agent who is always available to show your home to prospective buyers. These agents not only develop a sound marketing strategy, they implement it with control and confidence.

How long an individual has been in real estate isn't necessarily all you should look for. Experienced agents can grow jaded and rest on their laurels—and newer agents sometimes make up for a lack of experience with enthusiasm and effort. Make sure to do an apples-to-apples comparison.

The Friend and Relative

This one always baffles me. Sticking with the doctor theme; would you hire a doctor friend to do any medical procedure just because she is your friend? No! You would go for the most qualified for the procedure. Do the same when buying or selling a house. Friendship alone isn't enough to establish a professional's credentials. A true friend will understand and appreciate that this is a business decision. They will offer their credentials and expect to earn the business based on a strong résumé and plan, not because you passed notes back and forth in middle school or played on the high school football team together. Consider also how you would handle a problem or challenge that developed while selling your home and think if it is worth the risk of damaging a friendship or family relationship. Ask yourself if you can fire a friend or family member if they are not performing. Unless your relative is an all-star full-time agent who specializes in your area or has the right system to excel, he or she is unlikely to do as good of a job as another, qualified agent. That can breed resentment, as well as derail your goals. Ask yourself if you are willing to lose time, money, or both because your third cousin has a real estate license.

The Neighborhood Specialist or the Institution

Many believe that working with a neighborhood expert is especially important in areas where moving a block can raise or lower the value of a home by $100,000 or more. An agent who specializes in a neighborhood may also be in touch with buyers who are looking for a home just like yours, or sellers who haven't put their home on the market yet. All good things. Before christening them with the crown, find out what makes them an expert. Is it the most signs in yards, or the fact that they have a booth at the local farmer's market? Knowledge of the local market isn't only acquired by living in the immediate neighborhood. Sure, your agent should have intimate knowledge of recent sales, area features, schools, businesses, and so on, but that can be achieved through extensive research and grass-roots efforts. Convenience shouldn't be the primary reason for choosing an agent. It is simple to find out how many completed sales they have, what their closing rate and average days on the market are, or what their list price versus sale price is. Yes, they may have the most signs in the neighborhood, but finding out how many sold compared to languishing on the market is critical.

The same can be said for an agent who is "the institution." You know the type, the agent who's been in the market since the dawn of time and sold every home in the city three times. Yes, quantity is important, but only if the quality of service for today's consumer is still up to par and the veteran agent is not resting on past experiences. An experienced agent may have sold more homes last year or within the last decade than anyone else, but dig a little deeper. How many of their listings did not sell? How many were reduced over and over before they sold? How long were the houses on the market? How smoothly was the process handled? How accessible was the agent when there were questions or problems? How many more questions can I ask in a row? A long track record is worth more if there's proven value in it.

The Celebrity
The rise of reality TV has created a successful niche of agents who share their expertise on the small screen. Most have grown excellent businesses that allow for exposure not thought possible even

ten years ago. Unfortunately, this exposure is more often for the agent and not for the home or buyer. By the time an episode airs, the home has either been on the market for months or has been sold through traditional or nontraditional methods. Buyers don't care whose sign is in the yard; they care about the home they will buy. Fame can't force a buyer to buy because Tanner McShinyteeth was on primetime. This is good to know as a buyer OR seller. We are a media based society that is obsessed with celebrity. From the magazines in grocery checkout aisles to primetimeTV, we love our pop culture. Celebrity, though, does not equate to expertise. It can, but they do not go hand in hand. All celebrity generally equates to is celebrity. In speaking with some of my clients who previously wanted to work with celebrity agents, many became discouraged when they were passed off to less experienced support staff or teammates of the celebrity, simply because their home or goals were not high profile enough for the head honcho's personal attention.

Selling: The Post and Pray Realtor

The post and pray Realtor possesses several business traits that accurately reveal their ability to completely wing it. "Why spend money on marketing?" is how the post and pray Realtor thinks. This is the last thing you want as a seller who is looking to get top dollar for a home. A consistent example is a total disregard for the importance of good real estate photography. In fact, with most lousy real estate agents, this is one of the first things another Realtor will notice. This error in quality reflects poorly on them, on your home, and on you, the seller. There is nothing more true in real estate sales than the famous saying, "A picture is worth a thousand words." The photography of your home can make or break a sale. You are also just as likely to see from a bad Realtor an off center Xerox copy of a multiple listing service (MLS) sheet left in your home. Even well-established or luxury Realtors have been known to rely on the three Ps of Put a sign in the yard, Put the home on the MLS, and Pray. Post and pray agents see some success with this formula, and use it over and over again. If you are fortunate enough to be in a blistering hot seller's market where homes sell faster than ice cream cones on a hot summer day, then the MLS might be all you need. The majority of the time, however, this is not the case. When real estate markets are in balance or there is a decent supply of homes, you need every edge you can get when trying to sell.

There are some obvious red flags to avoid when selecting a Realtor. Red flags often form as a pit in your gut or a buzz in your head. They don't FEEL right. Here are several seemingly small and insignificant issues that can compound themselves into countless problems when selecting the wrong agent.

Showing Up Late or Unprepared

Showing up late, dressed poorly, and an overall lack of profession-alism are like nails on a chalkboard to me. When you look to sell your castle, often you will be paying an agent thousands of dollars. A million dollar home with a 3 percent listing commission would be $30,000 to the agent. Do you think this is enough incentive for an agent to show up on time and not wear a tank top and flip-flops? I love to be casual, but I don't expect anyone to pay me $30,000 to do it. If you work at a beach or resort community where board shorts are the norm, fine. You get the point. When meeting an agent for the first time, they should have:

- Requested initial information about your goals.
- Shared their process for your success and summarized your goals together.
- Explained how they will deliver on their promises.

When you meet with a financial planner, lawyer, or insurance pro-fessional, these are your expectations. The same goes for realty. Expect the prospective Realtor to be prepared with relevant market data of sales of comparable properties and actively marketed homes in your area. This information should be readily available and presented in a neat and organized manner. A snap judgment isn't good enough. You also need to determine if the agent is competent, and the best way to do that is to check up on references. Ask for references on *recent* sales—check up on references of *recent* customers. Find out how an agent's customers feel about their selling experience. If they are a newer agent, this can be fine. Get character references from their broker or manager.

Lack of Written Agreements

Imagine you want to remodel your master bathroom—new tile, in-floor heat, vanity with slow close drawers and marble tops, backsplash, dual sinks, and mirrors; the whole nine yards. A smart plan would be to get estimates from reputable remodelers and compare them based on price, time, quality, references, and the like. For an intricate job, you may find it difficult to accept the details of a bid verbally, let alone multiple bids. The same should be said about working with a Realtor. Inexperienced, shady, or mediocre agents will not bother to put their services in a written plan for fear of rejection, or even worse, accountability. This goes for both buyers and sellers. Without a signed agreement, an agent has no loyalty, disclosure, or confidentiality agreement in place with you. Yes, this could be bad news. Instead, with a few representation agreements to compare, you can get a feel for which professionals are more thorough and you can educate yourself regarding the costs and services associated with your transaction.

No Communication Skills

Study after study show that one of the biggest complaints homeowners have with their real estate agent is a lack of communication. As of this writing, 80 percent of home shoppers say they would use their agent again. Less than 20 percent actually do. For most agents, once a transaction is completed, it's on to the next paycheck. When you have a showing of your home, it is great to know what the buyer thought about it as well. A rockstar Realtor will have a good system in place to get feedback from the buyer's agent, or to gather additional information when you are interested in a home to purchase.

Additionally, the most important work of an agent is not to find the home or buyer, but to make sure the sale closes. For their client, that includes making sure the buyer is financially approved, the home is free of liens before it goes on the market, the appraisal or valuation is accurate, and issues raised by the home inspection are resolved. What happens with a lack of follow through? Oh, not much…just lost sales, missed opportunities, and life plans altered. Sad face. ☹

Absence of Financial Understanding
Proof-of-funds, preapproval, and prequalification can be three different things. The best agents understand how you will be making a home purchase financially, or what to look for in an offer from a buyer on your home. When you're preapproved or prove your ability to purchase, you have much more negotiating clout with the seller. The seller knows you can close the transaction because a lender has carefully reviewed your income, assets, credit, and other relevant information. In some cases, like multiple offers, being preapproved or having cash evidence in your agent's hands can make the difference between buying and not buying a home. The best deals move quickly, so like the Boy Scouts say, be prepared. An added benefit is you can save thousands of dollars as a result of being in a better negotiating situation. A good agent knows how to use this; a bad one doesn't think to ask. If you wait or are uninformed, you may run the risk of falling in love with the home of your dreams and losing it, all because of lack of preparation.

The Agent Suggests the Highest Price for Your House
Pricing a home too high at the start often means it takes longer to sell and ultimately sells for less. If you're too high for the market, buyers will not even look at it, because they know you're not

realistic as a seller. Unbeknownst to many home buyers and sellers, the Realtor does not set the market. We cannot produce buyers or force them to buy. Like stocks, bonds, fortunes, and pork bellies, the market sets the supply and demand. If you're selling your house, get listing information from a good agent that will prove what comparable homes have sold for in your area and how long they take to sell. Generally, all agents are looking at the same data, so the suggested listing price should be close if you speak with multiple agents. Perk up an eyebrow if you have a big outlier.

Too often, agents tell their sellers or prospects to list their home for higher than market value. Don't get me wrong; we are paid on commission. If I could, I'd like any seller we work with to sell for double the asking price. However, agents like to sell homes, not just list them. Generally, agents agree to list high either out of fear of losing the listing, wanting another sign in a yard to show market share as a loss leader, or because they're practicing the art of "buying" a listing. Telling a seller they can get X when the market says Y may sing the song a seller wants to hear and secure the contract for that agent. Then, as no offers come and the days on market tick on, the agent blames the market and frequently requests price drops until the home can sell. Sadly, these price drops often bring the home to less than the original value should have been. The longer your property sits on the market, the more people are going to think there's something wrong with it. This method is employed by shortsighted agents who are more interested in themselves than they are in you, and is an extremely poor strategy in selling a home at the highest possible price.

The Agent Charges a Lower Commission to the Buy Side
This is a fun topic that is always glossed over with sellers. In most areas, commissions are traditionally 5 to 7 percent, split approximately between the buying and selling agent. If the commission paid to other agents on your house is lower than area average, fewer agents will show it. Think of it like this; if an agent can show

her client home A paying a 1% fee and home B at 3%, where do you think they will gently prod their client? This doesn't mean you can't negotiate a slightly lower commission if one agent ends up both listing and selling the house. Everything is negotiable. Some newer companies rebate part of the commission to the buyer or seller, but don't use that as the sole reason to choose an agent. That's only a bargain if the agent is otherwise a good fit. We'll get deeper into this in upcoming chapters.

The Agent Isn't Well-Versed with Your Style of Property

If you're buying or selling a condominium, don't pick an agent who has no experience selling condos. If you're looking for investment property, find an agent who traditionally works with investors and knows how to read a pro forma. No matter what an agent may say, there are different skills developed for properties with homeowner associations, oceanfront, commercial, and the like. Many agents can and do have multiple specialties, but you want to make sure the agent is well-versed in the type of transaction you're doing. They don't have to be the Condo Queen or the Duplex Dude, but they should show you a skill set that increases your likelihood of success.

No One Will Notice

Occasionally, a home may have a flaw; a crack in the foundation, asbestos on older pipes, or maybe it was used as a meth lab. Defects like these obviously affect the sale and value of the home, and a seller may be motivated to hide a few facts to benefit. Don't ever do this. Not only should you avoid this practice, but run from an agent who would agree or suggest it. Anyone who lies *for* you will lie *to* you. Many communities require all sellers to fill out a property disclosure form that outlines all you know about your home. Your agent is prohibited from filling this out for you, but they should offer guidance on how to properly fill out the form. They should also suggest necessary repairs that should be made prior to putting the house on the market. If you don't do this, the now furious new owner of a former drug lab can sue you and possibly your agent, even years later, for lack of disclosure.

Not Using Available Resources

As you will see in this book, agents have SOOOOOOO many tools available to them to assist their clients, but the majority fail to use them properly, if at all. Internal marketing and educational tools from a brokerage, best practices from seasoned colleagues, professional organizations—all of these are assets that top performers in your market will tap into to improve their service offerings. Not using these and other advantages is a disservice to the buyers and sellers an agent tries to assist. Before selecting an agent, ask what resources he or she utilizes in marketing and client services.

The Last Word: All in all, avoid the underqualified, unresponsive, unprofessional, and inexperienced. Your pocketbook and sanity will thank you.

CHAPTER 2

Supply and Demand

"Teaching may be compared to selling commodities.
No one can sell unless somebody buys."
—John Dewey

I n this day and age, if you need a ride from place A to place B, you can pull out your phone and load up the Lyft or Uber app. Though the two ride-sharing companies advertise their differences, in reality, they are almost identical. If you have ridden them both, it's difficult to say that either is much better, or much worse, than the other. In most cities, they offer similar costs and service. For riders, this is great news. Two tech start-ups are fighting to give us better service at lower prices across the country.

The two driver services have become so synonymous that Uber has tried to poach Lyft's drivers in a mass recruiting effort. If Uber believes almost any Lyft ride can be easily transformed into an Uber ride, why shouldn't we just use Lyft? This is the basis for becoming a commodity.

When going through the home buyer or seller decision process, most people take several months to pinch and prod their minds into a formulated plan. Over this time, they will see a dozen or so agents, even if just subconsciously. The bus bench, an open house, online, billboard, coffee shop, cousin's friend's uncle's coworker—everyone is or knows an agent, it seems. To overcome this sea of agents, many sales professionals believe that by discounting their products or services during good or bad times, they can increase sales and maintain customer loyalty. However, what these folks are really doing is just the opposite, because they have turned their products and services into a commodity. Basic business rule: the price of your products and services is directly tied to the value your products or services provide your customers. A lack of differentiation or value creates a pricing war. Like dueling gas stations across the road from each other dropping unleaded prices, thousands of real estate practitioners can't or won't find a way to differentiate, leaving price as the only way to attempt to show value.

Diminishing value through commoditization is a trade characteristic that's been in the real estate industry for decades. Come on, there are two million of us! There's less of a need today for real estate agents who exist solely to provide consumers with information already available to them via the Internet. If it's just about opening the doors for home showings, this is something that surely doesn't warrant a big commission. The need for real estate agents who don't provide anything of true value is fading rapidly. This isn't to say that real estate agents aren't needed. They certainly are. Knowledgeable and professional agents offer a wealth of value. However, it is worth describing the differentiators that sort the haves from the have nots.

Some of the best businesses in the world are the most successful and adored by their client base because of a well-positioned differentiation among their competitors. Agents differentiate through a unique selling proposition (USP). What makes them better and different is providing a service experience that's truly unique. It grabs people's attention. It can't be easily copied. And it offers a clear-cut, marketable benefit to you. Some propositions practically jump out at you. Think Kleenex or Band-Aid instead of tissue or bandage. How did these products become synonymous with the term that describes them? The best agents will have differentiation as well. They will have analyzed their competition, determined what sets them apart, identified customer pain points and how to correct them, and offered services and guarantees that are unlikely to be paralleled in their market.

Think of it this way: what makes you choose one tennis shoe, airline, or grocery store over another? Chances are it's their success in defining their USP and broadcasting that message to the marketplace. They are able to focus and provide more services, faster, bigger, and/or better. Find the agent leaders who differentiate and offer more value; their star will shine brighter than the rest. These are practitioners who want to offer more than just "ordinary." They take the extra step to dedicate themselves and their businesses to improvement. They refuse to be merely mediocre. And because they want more, they generally get it.

In the business world, you'll come across people who are happy enough with just getting by and living a middle-of-the-road lifestyle. They do enough to meet the bills each week, but don't really make revolutionary contributions to their craft or the world as a whole. To put it simply, they exist. Agents who fit this description, with no definable system, no experience, and no distinguishable value, are just like the vast majority of agents out there. The agent is a commodity, to be traded and bartered at the lowest bid.

On the other hand, there are industry leaders dedicated to controlling their own success. We want to change the industry we are in, find exponential success, and be more than just another business owner. We know the future we want and dedicate ourselves to ensuring it becomes our and our client's reality. This work pays off for our clients most of all, who reap the benefits of our differentiation.

If you've ever been offshore fishing for blue marlin, you know that this six-hundred-plus-pound behemoth is one of the most difficult saltwater fish to catch in the world. Landing one requires tremendous skill and appropriate bait. Now, if I were to offer you two options for catching blue marlin—a fishing net or a precisely tuned outrigger-led fishing line with just the right blue marlin lure—which would you take? It seems like an obvious answer, but when you relate it to an agent looking to provide the best service and experience, it's amazing how many Realtors choose to go with the net when it comes to marketing and building their authority. Instead of putting something out there that their exact target market is desperate to have, they instead take a big ol' net and sling it as best they can into the water, hoping to wrangle up a big catch.

The Last Word: When an agent lacks flexible growth and differentiation, they join the masses as a commodity of discounting value and putting themselves in the position of Walmart, competing on price. To be that unique red dress at the cocktail party, a savvy agent will show you the actual results that would be considered valuable to you.

BOOK 2

Merriam, Wikipedia, and Beyond

CHAPTER 3

What's a Realtor?

"In a crowded marketplace, fitting in is a failure. In a busy market-place, not standing out is the same as being invisible."
—Seth Godin

I f we did a blind taste test on Starbucks coffee, do you think most people would tell us that Starbucks sells the best coffee in the world? Maybe. Either way, the taste of their various cups of Joe doesn't stop Starbucks from selling ocean beds full of coffee. It cannot be easy to take a simple product like coffee and make it a billion dollar revenue stream; if it were, everyone would be doing it. To its credit, Starbucks took a simple product and implemented a masterly level product plan.

Nolan Bushnell, the founder of Atari and inventor of Nolan's Law, stated that all the best games are easy to learn but difficult to master. They should reward the first quarter of players and the hundredth. Interestingly enough, real estate is the same way. With "everyone" making money flipping houses or selling million dollar listings on TV, it seems that real estate is so easy to learn; but look a little further behind the curtain. There are only so many that have truly mastered the game.

What does it take to become proficient in buying or selling property, or representing others to do so? As a prerequisite to selling real estate, a person must be licensed by the state in which they work, either as an agent/salesperson or as a broker. Before a license is issued, minimum standards for education, examinations, and experience as determined state by state must be met. Realtors, agents, brokers, and realty professionals; throughout this book I use these monikers somewhat interchangeably, but they are not the same. To give you an overview, let's break down a few definitional differences. In general, the titles you may come across include:

- **Real estate agent:** Anyone who earns a real estate license can be called a real estate agent. He or she may have a license as a sales professional, an associate broker, or a broker.
- **Realtor:** A real estate agent who is a member of the National Association of Realtors (NAR). This professional must adhere to the standards of the association and its code of ethics.
- **Real estate broker:** A person who has taken education beyond the agent level as required by state laws and has passed a broker's license exam. Brokers can work alone or they can hire agents to work for them.
- **Real estate associate broker:** Someone who has taken additional education classes and earned a broker's license but chooses to work under the management of a broker.

Generally, most people would describe a Realtor as the face of the industry. What does the average Realtor actually look like? Let's share a few statistics that NAR recently listed for their average member profile.

- The typical Realtor has twelve years of experience.
- Sixty-five percent of Realtors reported having a website for at least five years and are using social media.

- The typical Realtor earned 40 percent of their business from repeat clients or referrals from past clients and customers.
- Fifty-eight percent of all Realtors are female.
- A substantial majority of Realtors—85 percent—own their primary residence.
- Eighty-four percent of Realtors are certain they will remain in the business for two more years.
- The average Realtor is in a second career as a professional and several years past fifty in age.

In most areas, it is the Realtor who shares information on the homes they are marketing through the MLS. Working with a Realtor who subscribes to an MLS will give you many benefits over a real estate agent, like access to the greatest number of homes or ethical and legal obligations by being a member of a professional association. As mentioned, a Realtor is held to an even higher standard of conduct under NAR's code of ethics. In recent years, state laws have been passed setting up various duties for different types of agents, so find out if the practitioners you speak with are Realtors or just agents; the difference can be Grand Canyon wide. If you start working with a Realtor, ask for a clear explanation of your state's current regulations so you will know where you stand on these important matters.

Definitions aside, there is also a big service difference between buyer's and seller's agents. Until recently, the line separating the two was very thin. In fact, the traditional buyer's agent has a greater legal obligation to an individual selling a property than the one trying to buy it. As a buyer, the advantages of contracting with an exclusive buyer's agent are readily apparent. They have the ability to disclose inside information about the seller's position that the seller's agent cannot legally divulge. Such information can benefit the buyer when making an offer to purchase real estate. The buyer's agent can work for the lowest sale price while the seller's legally cannot. They are contracted with the seller. And importantly, a buyer will not be under pressure to purchase any particular property since all sales will be commissioned under the terms of an exclusivity contract. This means the way a buyer's agent is compensated is most often from the seller's side, allowing the agent's expertise to help a client comfortably negotiate the purchase and sales process.

As an example, suppose you sign an offer to buy a home for $850,000 and you go directly to the seller's agent. You really want the property, and there's a chance other offers are coming in, so you tell the listing broker, "We'll go up to $860,000 if we have to. But of course, don't tell that to the seller." Since you are dealing with a seller's agent, he or she may be duty bound to tell the seller that important fact. In most states, the seller's agent doesn't have any duty of confidentiality toward you. Honest treatment might dictate that the agent warn you that they must convey to the seller anything that would be useful, but there are no guarantees of this. We'll go over this in depth in Book 4.

Knowing the difference between the various types of practitioners and their roles and responsibilities to you will help you pick the right professional to work for you and your goals.

Specialization

Raise your hand if you'd rather work with a specialist or a generalist in any given field. As a car collector, my guess is you'd visit the specialist mechanic for your '57 Ford Fairlane, just as you may hire a wedding planner over a general event planner for your big day. It's not always an easy question to answer, mostly because both sides of the debate come to the table with some convincing arguments. The major trend among Realtors is to favor generalization as agents try to work with anyone and everyone. Is this really the best move, or are professionals better off going with a specialization strategy? In my opinion, most agents who are specialists are far more capable than agents who consider themselves generalists. We as consumers don't want to work with an agent who sells a few homes here and there if we are selling a twenty million dollar luxury loft in SoHo. A generalist pursues whatever whims occur, and although they may branch out further than a specialist, they are often a jack of all trades, master of none. A specialist has put the time and energy necessary into studying a topic to come close to mastering it, and this process develops other useful skills. Before I was seven years old, I contracted a stubborn ear infection, and the ailment caused me an emergency visit to the hospital. My parents took me to a general physician, where the doctor prescribed some medicine based on his initial diagnosis of the illness and his past experience. When the earache was persistent, other options were sought to address the pain. Traditional, tried and true methods were used. Zoom ahead to today, and my parents probably would have taken me directly to an otolaryngologist or other Ear, Nose, and Throat (ENT) specialist; they would not have chanced missing an expert opinion or better prescription for their child if it was available or needed.

Time and again in the business world, specialization is king. Economist Adam Smith got it started when he demonstrated the economic value of specializing tasks in a pin factory, and the subsequent improvements in speed and quality assurance. McDonald's basically invented fast food by specializing in their process of making burgers and fries. It doesn't take a business guru to understand why specialization makes the business world turn. Your car collector mechanic is probably full time and not a weekend warrior. Specialization wins. So that alphabet soup after the name of any professional, including agents, can be an indication that they have taken extra steps to become more proficient in their craft. Some of the best examples of professional specialization for agents include CRS (Certified Residential Specialist), ABR (Accredited Buyer's Representative), SRES (Seniors Real Estate

Specialist), and CLHM (Certified Luxury Home Marketing). Sadly, many practitioners don't allocate funds for education. This is backward thinking. As an agent, you take the class to acquire the skills to become more proficient, provide better service, and increase increase your sales and word of mouth. The skills agents learn and the referral relationships they develop with other students they meet will dramatically affect your bottom line and potential for success.

The Last Word: In making your decision to work with an agent, find out what differentiates them. It is important to have the most qualified person as your guide when making one of life's most rewarding and expensive commitments.

CHAPTER 4

Salespeople

"A-B-C; always be closing."
—Glengarry Glen Ross

There is a story about a young man from the Midwest who moves to Florida and visits a big "everything under one roof" department store looking for a job. The manager says, "Do you have any sales experience?"

"Yeah," the kid says. "I was a vacuum salesman back home."

Though unsure, the boss liked the gumption of the young man and offered him the job. His first day on the floor had its typical growing pains, but he seemed to work through it. After the store was locked up, the manager came down to the sales floor. "How many customers bought something from you today?"

The kid frowned, looked at the floor, and muttered, "One."

"Just one?! Our salespeople average twenty to thirty sales a day. Your effort will have to change, and soon, if you'd like to continue your employment here. We have very strict standards for our sales force. One sale a day might have been acceptable where you're from, but you're not on the farm anymore, son." The rookie took his beating well, which made the manager feel a little bad. He asked, somewhat sarcastically, "So, how much was your one sale for?"

The kid looked up at his boss and said, "$101,237.65."

The boss, astonished, spurted "$101,237.65?! What the heck did you sell?"

The shrugging kid explained, "Well, first, I sold him some new fish hooks. Then I sold him a new fishing rod to go with his new hooks. Then I asked him where he was going fishing and he said down the coast, so I told him he was going to need a boat, so we went down to the boat department and I sold him a twin engine Chris-Craft. Then he said he didn't think his Honda Civic would pull it, so I took him down to the automotive department and sold him that 4x4 Expedition."

The boss said, "A guy came in here to buy a fish hook and you sold him a boat and a TRUCK?!"

The kid said, "No, the guy came in here to buy tampons for his wife, and I said, 'Dude, your weekend's shot, you should go fishing.'"

Salesmanship is the art of selling products or services and more so, convincing customers to buy a *certain* product or service. In a competitive and modern world, the importance and utility of salesmanship has been increasing day by day. People don't want to be sold to, but they definitely love to buy. The best salespeople understand this and help convert human needs into human wants.

At heart, every real estate agent is a salesperson. We help people buy and sell homes, and our clients have much benefit of this. We help them drive prices up or down. We supply information to make buying or selling decisions. We express details of the market that affect timing of sales. This is a win–win–win; we make income, and buyers and sellers move to a new life. We all put money back into the economy. We enlist other professions, like moving companies and home inspectors, and that puts more money into the economy. If you want to get really deep, like spiritual guru Deepak Chopra deep, salesmanship contributes to the economic development of a society by increasing the standard of living, removing ignorance, and educating people regarding different types of products and their usefulness.

There is, of course, a dark side of the Force. Many people have a less positive opinion of traditional sales, viewing anyone in the profession as fast talking, pushy, and insincerely self-interested. If you Google "salespeople are…" you will get autofill options like "liars" and "sleazy." This perception is not always misguided; clichés are clichés for a reason. We or those we know have experienced a salesperson who has promised the moon and didn't deliver, or was overly aggressive and came across as only motived for his or her own goals. There was a queasy feeling imparted of, "I'll do or say anything to get the deal." This conflict of interest sits in your stomach like swallowed gum, a pit that doesn't go away until you leave the scene. We all want to avoid this. Fortunately, there is a better method for working with the right type of sales professional.

CHAPTER 5

The Cream of the Crop

"The people with the best advice are usually the ones who have been through the most."

—www.livelifehappy.com

I magine wanting to buy a car. As you walk into a car showroom, you are approached by a smiling employee. Before she can speak, you say, "Why yes, **you** can help me. What sort of car should I buy? How much should I pay for the best car for me?" Most of us can agree this would be a rare exchange. The reason is the same as when shopping at the mall or in any retail store, when a clerk or salesperson walks over and asks if they can help, we say, "I'm just browsing" or "No, thanks." We might actually need the help, but we don't want the hassle or pressure of being sold. We hate the pressure that comes with being put on the spot, someone invading our time or space without being invited. However, when making any decision or reaching for a goal, we do want advice. We don't want to reinvent the wheel or do something we have no practice at, skill with, or interest in. Instead, we would like answers from a reputable, proven source. This is the difference in our view of salespeople versus advisers.

As a licensed agent, there are several ethical responsibilities to uphold: obedience, loyalty, confidentiality, reasonable care, accounting, and disclosure. Think of these duties along the lines of attorney-client privilege. Though we as an industry are supposed to adhere to these ethical codes, like attorneys, not all agents are created equal. Many are willing to work in shades of gray when it comes to the standards of professionalism. Some agents will focus more on the sales side than the advising side, and vice versa, and there can be a fine line of differences. As a salesperson, you are only as good as your product, and more often than not, the product is the agent themselves. So, if your "product" is lousy, business is much more difficult. If you don't sell, you don't eat. Picture working with an agent who hasn't sold a home in a few months, and you get an idea of how important the sale is to that agent. If push comes to shove in that scenario, it is possible the agent may think about their own best interests more than yours. Home buyers or sellers seeking advice face an army of salesmen, many marching onward and looking for the next commission check.

Conversely, an adviser is a trusted resource, less susceptible to market conditions, and more likely to quote facts, risk assessment, and market trends to offer a cornucopia of solutions. If you truly are seeking objective advice, you should work with a Realtor who built their practice and services as an adviser, who will always act in your best interests. This is known as a fiduciary standard, which occupies a position of special trust and confidence between agent and client. This standard includes disclosure of how the adviser is to be compensated and any corresponding conflicts of interest. An adviser often educates, allowing home buyer and seller the peace of mind from knowing enough so as to avoid being the center of a feeding frenzy of salesmen. Think of it like this: CEOs, business owners, and celebrities surround themselves with managers, associates, and handlers who each play a specific role to make their lives more efficient. This system allows them to focus on what they are good at or passionate about. In essence, they surround themselves with people who are smarter than them. Often, these teams include attorneys, accountants, financial planners, office staff, and yes, real estate professionals. You can't be good at everything, so build a team of…wait for it…advisers.

Best practices can also range in scope of services. The best professional does not let a prospective client hire them until the client truly understands the full range of services offered so as to create the best game plan for success. A home buyer or seller will have a litany of variables to accomplish their goals, and the best adviser will tailor their services, dependent upon a detailed analysis of these objectives. A home buyer who does not share their method of purchase, time frame, and ideal home description, for example, is not going to make the best decisions or receive the best service from their agent. In a roughly thirty to sixty minute orientation, a reputable adviser will highlight goals and take the time to understand personality, prior relationships with agents, and insights on how the homeowner can work with their firm. If a homeowner has ever fired an agent or never had an adviser, the professional will find out why and establish dual expectations. What shall be the frequency of phone calls and meetings? What defines a search or marketing plan? What are alternative backup options if the original plan doesn't go as expected? For the window shopper, this will be a waste of time. For the serious home buyer or seller, this will be some of the best time spent over the course of their work with the agent. The foundation of a solid process is now built.

After orientation, the adviser prepares a specific written plan of goals and services that creates success for all parties. This plan breeds a well-informed client, not just a sold client. Advisers understand they are only as good as their loyal book of business, and they will up their game to provide a service to be proud of. A good adviser with a solid fan base also provides the home buyer or seller with a built-in list of references and endorsements that a typical salesperson does not have.

Surprisingly to most salespeople, the best aspects of service often come *after* a home has closed. Annual reviews, market updates, and consistent communication about the marketplace will provide you with all the tools needed to be a successful homeowner or seller, and hopefully avoid mistakes similar to the ones made prior to the recession. As a dual benefit, having a high-touch relationship with your agent will develop further rapport to understand potential future wants and needs, helping you anticipate a best plan of action, time line, and how to make the most of the market. Like an insurance agent or even your local hairdresser, once your agent understands your goals, they can further build upon the benefits they offer you.

The Last Word: Professional advice can be very helpful in working toward your home goals and knowing the advice you're given is in your best interest, which provides peace of mind. So ask yourself, "Am I working with an adviser or a salesperson?" If the answer is the latter, it might be time to reconsider. A healthy balance gives the best of both worlds.

BOOK 3

Characteristics
of the Best Realtors

One of the oddest things about the story of Arnel Pineda is that it's not actually quite as odd as it might seem.

Growing up in the Philippines, Pineda's parents entered him in many singing contests. His mother and father were both tailors, and Arnel knew that when his dad walked toward him with a tape measure, it meant new clothes for another competition.

As a young adult, Pineda was a bar and club singer well known for singing cover band material. Working in Manila in 2007, he received an e-mail from Neal Schon, the guitarist from Journey. While searching for a new lead singer, Schon had seen videos of Pineda performing on YouTube and contacted Noel Gomez, a longtime fan and friend of Pineda, to ask for Pineda's contact information.

Pineda initially dismissed the e-mail as a joke and didn't believe he was talking to a founding member of one of the biggest bands in rock history. But after being persuaded by Gomez, he finally replied to Schon's e-mail. Ten minutes later, Pineda received a phone call from Schon, and soon thereafter, booked a flight to the United States. After spontaneously singing a Journey song for Philippines immigration officers to prove the reason for his trip, Pineda arrived in San Francisco to meet with Journey. Within a few songs, he had secured the job. From Journey fan to Journey member because of YouTube. In an interview soon after Pineda joined the band, Neal Schon said, "We feel reborn. I think there's a lot of chemistry among the five of us. At first, we were going to go into the studio and just write songs, but now it's escalated to a lot of great new and diverse material. The stuff sounds tremendous. Everyone's so stoked about it. We feel very fortunate to have found Arnel."

In every facet of life, diamonds in the rough are there to be discovered; to find them, one must look using nontraditional methods. To do the unique, sometimes you must try the unique. So how do you find the unicorn that is a real estate rockstar, worth their weight in gold?

CHAPTER 6

Industry Ripe for Change

"Progress is impossible without change, and those who cannot change their minds cannot change anything."

—George Bernard Shaw

I f you take a close look at the real estate industry, you will see that it has grown complacent. Even though technology and consumer acceptance have grown with instant information access, the real estate industry has struggled to keep up with the changing tide. New, potentially disruptive technologies such as automated agent selection and virtual home staging are all happening, but these innovations are not at the level of overtaking the trade. Many agents are still using 1990 or older methods, with fax machines, written purchase agreements, and hard copy day planners. In short, practitioners have not adopted innovation as much as possible and are lagging behind the best available options for their clients. It is time to turn this lag on its head.

The answer, like finding Arnel Pineda, merely requires a different lens with which to look through. The rockstar Realtor for you will be one who addresses the pain points in home buying and selling and asks the age-old question, "Is there a better way that will help to make life easier and better, and in the process, inject real change for my clients?"

While the full impact of the digital revolution on real estate has yet to be seen, there is a strong movement toward empowering the consumer. With people being able to access the data they need to make more informed decisions, the need for a less-informed middleman is scaling back. Smart real estate agents will embrace these technological advances and use them to survive, while others will woefully cling to their brochures and Rolodexes, lamenting that the old ways are better because that's the way things have always been done. Unfortunately, though, as history has shown time and again, nostalgia is rarely a good business model.

CHAPTER 7

Knowledge

"Knowledge is knowing that a tomato is a fruit; wisdom is not putting it in a fruit salad."

—Miles Kington

A very important thing to understand about the success of any professional is what comes from the knowledge and wisdom they have acquired in the practice of their trade. In his book *Outliers*, Malcolm Gladwell explains that it takes roughly ten thousand hours of practice to achieve mastery in a field. Gladwell studied the lives of extremely successful people to find out how they achieved success. Let's look at a few of his examples.

Bill Gates and Paul Allen dropped out of college to form Microsoft in 1975. Prior to starting the future software giant, Gates and Allen had thousands of hours of programming practice. First, the two cofounders met at Lakeside, an elite private school in the Seattle area. The district raised three thousand dollars to purchase a computer terminal for the school's computer club in 1968. A computer terminal at a university was rare in the 60s; Gates had access to a terminal in eighth grade. Gates and Allen quickly became addicted to programming, spending as many waking hours as possible in the lab. Additionally, the Gates family lived near the University of Washington, where Gates' father worked. As a teenager,

Gates fed his programming addiction by sneaking out of his parents' home after bedtime to use the university's computer. Gates and Allen acquired their 10,000 hours at a young age. When the time came to launch Microsoft in 1975, the two were ready.

In 1960, while they were still an unknown high school rock band, the Beatles went to Hamburg, Germany, to play in the local clubs. The acoustics, paycheck, and audiences were all subpar, but the band was able to log hundreds of hours of stage time—nonstop hours of playing time that forced them to get better. As the Beatles grew in skill, audiences demanded more performances…and thus more playing time. By 1962, they were playing eight hours per night, seven nights per week. By 1964, the year they burst onto the international scene, the Beatles had played over 1,200 concerts together. By way of comparison, many bands today don't play live 1,200 times in their entire career.

Everyone reading this book has achieved a certain station in life. Some may be CEOs, while others are just starting out. Whichever you are, here is something to think about. If I took all your possessions and money, within five years, you could get it all back again. Why? Because you know how to get where you are today. And you would probably get there faster because you now have the knowledge. You don't have to relearn that station in life because you've already lived it.

The elite don't just work harder than everybody else. At some point, the elite fall in love with practice to the point where they want to do little else. This passion creates a knowledge base that others cannot replicate. The elite violinist is the musician who spends all day plucking chords, and after leaving work, she listens to instructional podcasts on her ride home. The elite basketball player is the guy who spends all day on the court with his teammates, and after practice, he goes home to watch game films. The elite agent is the Realtor who networks, markets, and sells all day, and goes home to practice negotiation scripts or review housing trends. The elite are in love with what they do, and at some point, it no longer feels like work.

At times, this passion can border on the maniacal. At twenty-two, I was a technology consultant by day, budding property investor by night. I would work nights and weekends on a dump of a house a few buddies and I had purchased to try our first "flip." That same year, we also bought our first duplex, living on one side while other college friends lived in the other, their rent paying the entire mortgage. Instead of living for free, we took the saved rental funds and bought a second rehab property. Over the next decade, I would go on to become a national apartment firm's renovation leasing consultant, a licensed general contractor, and a property investor, and start my own property management company, title insurance company, and realty team. I have been in thousands of homes and I understand a house inside and out. I can easily work inside or outside the box to come up with solutions for any challenge a house buyer, seller, or investor may need assistance with. I have my 10,000 hours in spades; the best agents are like this. They put in their time, improving their skills like a hobby.

Business is tough, and barriers to entry and competition seem to only get more challenging. Yet even in the midst of a fragile economy, there are individuals and companies that prosper beyond all expectations. Practical knowledge plays a major role in success. I have worked with several investors who have made millions in real estate over the years, largely unaffected by the ebbs and flows of a recently volatile market. Tax changes, mortgage meltdowns, drops in values, changing credit limits…none of it matters. These successful investors have thousands of hours in the trenches of real estate practice. They have been there, done that in almost every possible scenario. Nothing scares them, for they have solved the Rubik's Cube of investing.

Rich Dad Poor Dad is a book written by Robert Kiyosaki and Sharon Lechter, based on Kiyosaki's life and the experiences he had in relation to two important men that played major roles in shaping his philosophies. The book advocates the importance of financial independence and building wealth through investing of all types, starting and owning businesses, as well as increasing one's financial and business intelligence and skill. One of the main principles the authors portray is the value of learning, of taking your practiced experiences and intentionally applying them to your success. The book also happened to be the game changer that the man on the shuttle bus referenced to me and my cohorts decades ago, and has been one of the early tomes I have embraced as a foundational pillar in my choice to make a career of real estate. Like Gladwell, Kiyosaki and Lechter highlight the immeasurable value of knowledge as a basis of success.

More than just years in a career, diligent practice and a mastering of a craft offer huge benefits to the clients we work with toward their goals. This muscle memory, this knowledge, provides a confidence in the ability to perform and to work through any challenges that may arise. An agent with a large knowledge base exponentially increases your success rate in all you want to accomplish with a home or property.

CHAPTER 8

Education, Expertise, and Authority

"Who you know only gets you in the door; what you know gets you the keys to the house."
—Gina Greenlee

The school of hard knocks has expensive tuition. Yes, knowledge is power, but how this knowledge is *applied* is where the real strength comes from. You can have knowledge about something without being an expert in it, but specialized knowledge, skill, and expertise in something allows one to perform at a high level.

Doctors, for example, are considered experts in medicine and health. Your cousin might have watched a lot of YouTube videos and read articles online, but would you really trust her to start rifling around your body if you are not feeling well? If the answer is yes, I can't help you. If the answer is, "God no, Jenny isn't getting anywhere near my blocked artery," then good; we are on the same page.

In business, who do you think customers trust more? Somebody who is knowledgeable, or somebody who has expertise? Expertise implies specific and encompassing knowledge of a particular subject, the application of which also relies on a variety of skills. That's an important distinction to make. Experts in their field can approach a problem with a set of skills that are not only applicable, but interchangeable. If their approach doesn't work at first, they are equipped to look at a challenge differently; they think laterally.

Generally, you hire an expert to do something specific, usually something you can't do yourself to the proper degree—like sell or buy your home (I'm sorry, I had to). There are tools out there that allow you to advertise online or view homes, but unless you have some sort of unprecedented natural local market knowledge, negotiating skills, legal forms, vendor relationships, home assessment knowledge, and on and on, your effort won't ever compare with that of a true expert. I say "true expert" because there are many, many people out there who will wave their knowledge around and call themselves experts when in reality they aren't.

There are over one million members of the National Association of Realtors, over two million licensed agents in the country (commodity alert!), and in my dealings, I find that most of them do not know how to manage their practices correctly. All of them are competing for the same business, and most of them do a very poor job of standing out from the crowd and displaying more value than the next. Very few call clients or prospects back quickly, and some don't call at all. Most do not think long term about their careers, and very few have a plan. Since this career is so unique and offers so much, "winging it" can have serious consequences for the practitioner, and worse, for you, the client.

Educational requirements for reputable professions can vary, but generally have a lengthy instruction or scholastic period. Lawyers, engineers, and doctors may top many people's lists. For those and similar careers, think of the amount of schooling required. Beyond high school, beyond undergraduate, there are years of extended study and practical apprenticeships, interning, residencies...these professionals are well educated in their field. This said, you may wonder what it takes to become a real estate agent. Depending on the state or country, not much. Visit any state's commerce department or board of realty website to see requirements. For most states, to be eligible to become a licensed real estate salesperson or agent, you must:

1. Be at least eighteen or nineteen years old.
2. Have legal US residency.
3. Complete your required prelicense education (number of hours required depends on the state, but most are around ninety).
4. Pass your state real estate license examination.

Hold the phone. Be an adult with a pulse, take three to four weeks of classes, and pass a test. What? Someone can meet this criteria and walk into my home? Isn't a home or property one of the largest investments most people will ever make in their lives? It may be worth a moment to find out your agent's credentials and see if they are a fit for your particular goals before signing on the dotted line. Look for evidence that an agent can show they have a higher degree of professionalism. Since most agents work off of referrals for a large portion of their business, we often just take our friend or coworker's word for the viability of an agent. You have to be particularly careful in identifying the people and businesses you can trust to actually deliver on what you want. Here are some of the best methods:

1. Look them up online. Agents will often post testimonials themselves, so make sure you check that their references are legitimate. Beyond that, people will often also write independent reviews. Make sure you check for those too, because a business isn't going to display any negative reviews of themselves.
2. Discover examples of their work. Take a look at the people they have worked with and see what you think of their efforts and whether you really want to invest

money in their services. Find their level of expertise, and if they have the skills to teach a class on their business or industry; often the devil's in the details.

3. Find out what memberships they have and networks they have fostered or belong to. An agent with a 10,000-person database that they communicate with regularly will have more branding, marketing, and reviews than someone with none.

4. Make sure you can communicate with each other effectively. It may seem silly, but it doesn't matter how skilled somebody is if you can't communicate your needs and have them listen, and vice versa. So meet with them, talk about your specific goals, and listen carefully to what they say. Does their approach fit with what you need? When you talk to them, do you find yourself listening to them and do they listen to you? Can they adapt sufficiently to your situation? Not sure? Then they haven't tried hard enough to win your business. Move on.

5. Ask for certifications. There are dozens of designations a Realtor can acquire to become an expert in a specific niche. Like those with a DDS, PhD, or MD, an educated agent will have acquired more tools in the mental toolbelt.

Though perception does not an expert make, it is a powerful force in shaping our opinions. Be wary of the agent with "perceived expertise." Any agent who tries to deceive customers in any way has a business that is doomed to failure, but they may take a few clients' home goals down the drain with them. You probably will get caught out at least once in life by somebody who talks a big game but can't deliver. You live and learn, and hopefully you'll be able to find an actual expert to do the thing you wanted done in the first place. Just recognize the force in your perceptions and how it can affect your opinion.

The entertainment industry is a great example. Hollywood is a place filled with glitz and glamour, fame and fortune, where the stars align. In truth, Hollywood represents a world of make believe. Music videos are shot at angles making the crowd look massive, no matter the venue. Managers and agents buy Twitter followers and Facebook likes for the clients they want more exposure for. People lie about things every day in order to evoke a better persona.

Perception is not reality, so finding other indicators of educational and experiential ability in an agent are necessary. Here is a little test; if I were to ask who the local expert is in real estate, what would you say? Who would come to mind in your town? In positioning, we see the experts as the perceived best. The blow-your-own-horn method is the most popular *incorrect* method of expressing expertise, and it is rampant in the real estate industry. It seems like everyone has received postcards, e-mails, business cards, or seen signs that share all the homes an agent has sold, why or how they are number one, or how long they have been in the business. But none of this proves expertise, leadership does. Leaders are always known and can demonstrate value. At one time, there was no Hilton, BMW, or Tiffany. Each of these companies created a positioning strategy against their competitors to become number one in their respective industries. Even though many copycats have come along, these companies maintain the perception and reality that they are the experts. The commonality is they became well known, most by some form of advertising and displaying excellent service. Your agent should be able to show value beyond basic services. Introducing you to a great moving company or mortgage broker, sharing what is trending in kitchen remodels, or passing on a great handyman or painter reference are little examples of a bigger picture. There must always be a benefit linking expertise and the product or service to the needs of the customer.

With all the information available directly to home buyers and sellers in today's digital world, it is easy to question why it is still important to choose a knowledgeable real estate agent. There are so many different situations—foreclosures, short sales, tenancy issues, new construction, litigation, service differences for different generations—that need working out. For the expert agent, these varied and often complex situations create opportunities. Agents need to invest the time to understand how these issues operate and how to manage them for their clients. You can't speak generally about any real estate market without recognizing that it is really dozens of micromarkets, which vary significantly in terms of how they performed last year and will continue to perform. The best real estate agents recognize this and change with the times to offer deep market knowledge to their buyers and sellers. You can't find that on a website on the Internet.

An expert is defined as, "One who has special skill or knowledge; a specialist." By this definition, would a certified public accountant (CPA) be an expert accountant? Do CPAs know more than regular accountants? Some do, and some probably don't. However, there is a perception that because of the extra training a CPA completes and the testing to receive the designation, that person might do a better job with your expenses and tax advice. Whether this is true in reality depends on the CPA. Passing tests does not make expertise. The real definition of an expert is a person who you can feel confident discussing a subject with and will place great weight on their advice. The real perception lies with the observer, not the expert. You are an expert and an authority if people say you are.

Before he retired, my father was an appliance salesma... ahem, an appliance adviser, selling high-end home appliances. This was a new career for him; he didn't know the first thing about being an adviser. He had experience from a previous life in *servicing* appliances, but never had to sell anything in his professional life. What did he do to learn? He went to classes and started talking to other salesmen and advisers. He asked to watch them "on the floor." He asked them how they spoke to prospects and offered them value, how they secured a commitment to buy, how they followed up. In short, he became a student of the industry. He found successful people who were doing what he wanted to do. He found experts, and became one himself.

The real estate profession is constantly changing, and the best real estate professionals stay abreast of those changes by continuing their growth and education. Expertise creates innovation. The more an agent knows, the more they can have an impact on your goals because they will be able to see things that less knowledgeable people can't see. These successes only increase the level of authority and mastery an agent has. Here is a perfect example, imagine trying this test. Send several letters to the editors of your local papers. Explain to them the type of business you are in and what you do. Let them know that if there are stories pertaining to that industry, you would be happy to provide them with any relevant information about the industry they may need. The editor generally will file this information; the one thing a reporter with a deadline doesn't want to do is research. They want a qualified source of information, an industry authority they can tap into and run with. Having that letter on file when a related story comes up, who do you think they are going to call? That's right; you. You have special knowledge about that industry. If you are quoted, the expertise you show will demonstrate the paper's expert source and point of view. Additionally, being in the business you wrote to the editor about, you are probably going to have advance knowledge of industry news before mainstream media will. Information usually circulates within an industry before it finds its way outside that industry. So you can be the one to "alert the media" to a newsworthy change in your industry. And you will more than likely be quoted as the source of the information.

Most business people, for some reason, don't appreciate all the time and study it took to learn their craft. They don't feel special for doing it. They sometimes assume that because they did it, anyone can. They feel uncomfortable charging customers a fair price for something that comes so easily to them. Experts have learned and have practical experience others don't have and don't want to learn. I could probably learn to concrete my driveway, but I don't want to. I'm going to call someone who has the skills to do that job.

Choosing a leading authority in the field and verifying their great amount of applied expertise is valuable. A Nobel Peace or Pulitzer Prize winner could be trusted as an expert in their field. You fully believe in the authority of their professional subject matter. If you have a heart condition, you'd rather take advice from a cardiologist than from a grocery delivery driver. One is an expert on the topic, one is not. The smart agent doesn't wait until they are forced to learn a concept or trend. The smart agent is in a constant learning mode, which only increases the benefits to their clientele. Experts have a point of view and are usually prepared to back up those points of view with facts and statistics of some kind. It's been twenty years since I sat in a college classroom, but I still attend four or five seminars or conferences on various realty topics each year. I probably read twenty books and pamphlets on real estate, service, and property marketing each year. Before expanding my operations into a new market, I would take the time to visit and flush out the services of my soon to be competitors. I would record the things I liked and the things I don't like about each one. I can then incorporate all the positives I found and eliminate all the negatives to begin a successful business.

Here is a brief overview to explain further. A potential client typically comes forward from our website, sign, referral network, or database of contacts. She first receives a reply in the form of an e-mail, call, text, or letter, usually accompanied by one or several of our gifts of value, like reports, guides, or booklets. We follow up. We take the initiative to book a consulting appointment over the phone or at the office. She may be told of or sent a pre-appointment checklist to review. We meet, and before day's end, she is asking me to come up with a plan of action—which I do. And nine out of ten times, it is accepted. This is the power of authority.

When you combine expert status, authority, and celebrity, you cash in a winning trifecta ticket. These three factors, working in concert, act to deliver three very desirable benefits: you are made able to readily attract more and better clients/customers, make selling to them easier, and make price less of an issue so that the profitability of your business improves.

CHAPTER 9

Crystal Balls and Tarot Cards

"Those who have knowledge, don't predict; those who predict, don't have knowledge."

—Lao Tzu

Supposed experts and authorities in their field often get asked for their opinions. Sadly, the experts are not always right. Ben Bernanke, former chairman of the Federal Reserve, was quoted as saying, "The Federal Reserve is not forecasting a recession." He said this in January of 2008…before the greatest economic collapse since the Great Depression.

In certain areas of the world, it is common to participate in small talk about basic shared experiences, like weather, sports, or politics. As a Realtor, I have probably been asked a thousand times, "How's the market?" I generally say, "It's phenomenal!" Because it is, depending on the facet or sector you are asking about. When one market is up, another is down, and so on. There are many ways to answer that question, but first we must know if there is a definitive way to know where the market is going. The answer is probably not. No one has a crystal ball, and Nostradamus never became a real estate agent. However, there are ways we can analyze the market and make educated guesses to put our clients in the best position for current and future success. Past experiences, classes, conferences, seminars, and water cooler education offer real estate agents ideas about how real estate trends are changing. Here is a further look at how a good Realtor can analyze the present to help predict the future for you.

Let's start by defining "the market." The real estate market is a term used to describe the overall economic state of real estate, based largely on the basic economic concepts of supply and demand. When supply is up, prices generally go down. When supply is down and demand is up, prices generally go up as well. This sounds simple enough, but the perception of "the market" is a bit more complicated than that. There are many different factors it can be referring to. The area of the country or world, end user, type of building, banking, political, and employment environments are just a few of the many influencers that press upon a real estate market's being stable or volatile. A renter in Iowa is going to want to know about a very different market than a rancher in Texas or a high-rise condo buyer in Miami. We need to know the who, what, why, when, and where.

There will always be an ebb and flow to real estate. A good friend of mine wrote his graduate school thesis on residential real estate value patterns since the late 1800s in the United States. He found that many areas of the country revolve around fourteen-year high and low cycles. His research stated that homes generally double in value every fourteen years, but also experience a depression of sorts. This number may change market to market, but you get the point. Ebb and flow, high and low. Think savings and loan debacle of the 1970s, Reagan-era tax reform of the 80s, and tech bubble of the late 90s and early 2000s. Realtors can be aware of these patterns and the fact that history often repeats itself. This pattern tracking gives us a leg up in predicting outcomes and trends. It is by no means consistent or precise, but watching patterns allows a professional to see outliers and share possible outcomes.

Like the highs and lows of the above examples, the market typically moves through four phases before repeating them again. As noted in a Harvard blog post by entrepreneur Teo Nicolais, those phases can be defined as follows.

Phase 1 is Recovery. Really, Phase 1 could be the beginning or the end. It's a chicken or the egg conversation; which comes first, recovery or recession? For the sake of argument, we'll start with recovery. It's the moment that the market stops declining and slowly starts to level off or grow again. If you think of a bell curve, this is the beginning of the bell, the flat point at the bottom.

During a recovery, you can expect to see vacancy rates stabilize. There is generally a lack of supply, because builders, developers, and contractors have been on hold for an extended period during the previous downturn. There are not enough homes or apartments being built to keep up with a slow but steady growth in demand. This is good; it is signaling the end of a declining market.

As a homeowner, buyer, or seller, you may want to know if it is a good time to move. Again, this depends on who's asking. As a home buyer, yes, absolutely, buy now! It is the bottom of the market, and there is "blood in the streets," as J.D. Rockefeller so famously said. Fear is instilled in much of the general population during this time, and most people are apprehensive to invest in real estate. However, during this time, it is great to buy properties for cash flow (think of the mantra buy low, sell high.) or really, any reason. Property values will continue to climb, so buying a first home, a vacation home, or investment property during recovery will be a huge equity or profit builder. From 2011 to 2016, some markets increased 40 to 50 percent in value. Think of buying a depressed home for $500,000, and five years later, it is worth $750,000. Where do I sign up for that? In 2010, that's where.

Phase 2 is Expansion. Expansion is a very exciting time in the real estate market cycle because the economy is starting to ramp up again. New construction takes place, and businesses are adding employees. People are becoming more confident in real estate again.

During this phase, home prices begin to rise because of the increase in demand. Remember previously, during recovery, there was not enough construction to keep up with supply requirements. As businesses and population needs expand, the price for commercial buildings will also increase. The expansion period is a great time to invest in real estate. Prices are rising, rent is going up, and people in general are more optimistic about the future.

As a homeowner, if the timing is right for you, this is a great time to sell. Although all of this prosperity sounds wonderful, a major problem is looming on the horizon. Property values can hit their peak at the end of this cycle. Therefore, those who sell during this time will receive huge profits, while those who buy will ride an upward wave until the end of the phase, when most likely, over-payment begins. As a seller, you probably will need a place to live, so make sure you think through all the logistics of selling high and trying to buy low. The best way to do this would be when down-sizing, selling non-owner occupied property, or moving to another area that is not in the same phase.

Phase 3 is Hypersupply. This phase is known as the boom time in the real estate market cycle. In the mid-2000s, US housing values increased by 89 percent from 2000 to 2006. Eighty-nine percent! Spoiler: It's not sustainable. Skyrocketing prices, mass building projects, and speculation dominated the housing landscape. Developers with no experience start popping up to get a piece of the action. In hypersupply, everyone wants to invest in real estate, and buying becomes a hot thing to do.

This period is caused by builders who are willing to pay more for land and construction than they should. Unfortunately, they base their predictions on the belief that rent or values will continue to rise. Demand during this time begins to level off, and you'll notice a flip as supply now outweighs demand. Vacancy rates start to increase, and though new construction is still occurring, the absorption of new homes begins to slow down. Employment also starts to trickle as many companies already expanded during Phase 2.

During hypersupply, home buyers will want to be more cautious about their buying strategies. Length of ownership, possibly value additions, and current interest rates can all play a part in decision making. In past hypersupply cycles, people suddenly thought that buying real estate was the quick way to get rich. Tread lightly during this phase. If you are a home owner or landlord during this time, selling marginal properties before the market starts to decline even more can be a great spring cleaning.

Phase 4 is Recession. Cue up the scary *Jaws* music again. During a recession, vacancy rates increase, employment decreases, and income declines as well. Foreclosures skyrocket, and people start to find themselves underwater. New construction slowly comes to a halt, and people begin to panic. As a result, rental rates will actually go down, since fewer people are willing and able to pay as much for units. Luckily, after the real estate market bottoms out in this phase, it will head upward into recovery, beginning the real estate market cycle once again.

Interestingly, the savviest investors actually look for "the bottom," since demand dips below supply, and great deals are to be found. During a recession, smart real estate agents will suggest you invest in properties that provide a strong cash flow. While your value will not increase anytime soon, you can still jump on some fantastic deals to help save the economy and pad your wallet. Then, in the near future, appreciation will climb aggressively as we begin Phase 1 again.

As agents, we have consistent access to this information and are surrounded by it daily. We have the ability to draw conclusions about when the best time is to buy and sell. Though no one can predict the real estate market with complete accuracy, great Realtors help clients recognize the phases within the cycle in order to help them build and keep an enormous amount of wealth. During each phase, Realtors can definitely feel the effects of which way the real estate market is headed. When an agent's phone is ringing and there is an increase in home showings, we are generally likely to be optimistic. Interestingly, there is a strong correlation between the collective confidence of Realtors and predictions regarding the housing market. Studies even show that Realtor confidence is an indicator of where the market is headed.

How best to utilize this wealth of information is the question. Exact timing is a crapshoot, but here are a few trends for the next few years as of the writing of this book.

Timing: Thousands of would-be sellers and buyers are agonizing over how they can time their next sale or purchase to coincide with the pop of this housing bubble, either by selling soon for optimal profit or swooping in with cash to pounce on post-pop pricing. True, the bust of 2007–2008 was a loud and robust one, but don't look for anything catastrophic this time. The present froth is being fueled by narrow supply and widespread demand, stringent credit policies, and false appreciation. Most real estate cycles don't explode like the last one; they just deflate slowly. Property and land continue to be reliable long-term investments, prone to usually modest peaks and valleys, done on a deal-by-deal basis, and subject to local economies. Remember, no one is making more dirt.

Coming out of a recession, we see healthy growth in home sales and prices, but at a slower pace than in the previous years. This slowdown is not an indication of a problem—it's just a return to normalcy. We've lived through fifteen years of truly abnormal trends, and after working off the devastating effects of the housing bust, we're finally seeing signs of more normal conditions. Distress sales will no longer be playing an outsized role, new construction will return to more traditional levels, and prices will rise at more normal rates consistent with a balanced market.

Generations of people: Representing almost two million sales, which is more than one-third of the total sales in the United States, are Millennials. This pattern will continue as their large numbers and improving personal financial conditions will enable enough buyers between ages twenty-five and thirty-four to move the market—again. The majority of these buyers will be first-timers, but that will require other generations to also play larger roles. Think ripple effect.

Two other generations will also affect the market: financially recovering Gen Xers and older Boomers thinking about or entering retirement. Since most of these people are already homeowners, they'll play a double role, boosting the market as both sellers and buyers. Gen Xers are in their prime earning years and thus able to relocate to better neighborhoods for their families. Older boomers are approaching or already in retirement and seeking to downsize and lock in a lower cost of living. Together, these two generations will provide much of the suburban inventory that millennials desire to start their own families. Assuming that most of these households will both sell and buy, it is important to recognize that this is shaping up to be the best run in recent memory to sell. Supply remains very tight, so inventory is moving faster. Given the forecast that price appreciation will slow to a more normal rate of growth, delaying a sale will not produce substantially higher values, and any new purchase will also have higher mortgage rates.

Higher mortgage rates will affect high-cost markets the most: Experts predicted that mortgage rates would go up, and they did—but they also went back down. Expect similar volatility, but the move by the Federal Reserve to guide interest rates higher should result in a more reliable upward trend in mortgage rates.

Higher rates will drive monthly payments higher, and debt-to-income ratios will also increase. Markets with the highest prices will see that increased rates will result in fewer sales; however, across the United States, the effect will be minimal, as the move to higher rates will spur more existing homeowners to sell and buy before rates go even higher.

Already unaffordable rents will go up more than home prices: The housing crisis has shifted so that the cost of rental housing is debilitating in most of the country. More than 85 percent of US markets have rents that exceed 30 percent of the income of renting households. Rents are also accelerating at a more rapid pace than home prices, which are normalizing. Because of this, it is more affordable to buy in most of the United States. However, for the majority of renting households, buying is not a near-term option due to poor household credit scores, limited savings, and lack of documentable stable income of the kind necessary to qualify for a mortgage today. Curses! This trend does not bode well for the health of the housing market in the future. It will only improve if we see more construction of affordable rental housing as well as more of a pathway for renters to become homeowners.

Builders will focus on more affordable price points: One aspect of housing that has not recovered yet has been single-family construction. Facing higher land costs, limited labor, and worries about depth of demand in the entry-level market, builders have shifted to producing more higher-priced housing units for a reliable pool of customers. That focus caused new home prices to rise much faster than existing home prices. Builders were able to be profitable and grow by following this move-up and luxury strategy, but their growth potential was limited by avoiding the entry level. That should begin to change. Credit access is slowly improving enough to make the first-time buyer segment more attractive to builders. Consumers of all types should consider new homes, but availability will be highly dependent on location.

The Last Word: Though Nostradamus never signed a purchase agreement, it is important to consult the real experts, so as to identify opportunities for the best time to buy and sell for your unique situation.

CHAPTER 10

Adversity

"That which does not kill us makes us stronger."
—Friedrich Nietzsche

I n his search for the perfect materials to create the lightbulb for common use, Thomas Edison tested thousands of different substances as filaments and sent men all over the world to try to find better materials. At one point during his search, an *American Magazine* reporter asked him if he had failed and how many times. Edison was quoted in the magazine as saying, "After we had attempted thousands of experiments on a certain project without solving the problem, one of my associates, after we had conducted the crowning experiment and it had proved a failure, expressed discouragement and disgust over our having failed to find out anything. I cheerily assured him that we had learned something. For we had learned for a certainty that the thing couldn't be done that way, and that we would have to try some other way." In essence, Edison and his associate had found thousands of ways NOT to make a lightbulb. This glass half full view of success led to the creation of electric light, as well as many other popular inventions still used today. Disappointment did not lead to quitting; rather, for Edison, it created another step down the tunnel of success. If at first you don't succeed, try, try, again. For him, failure was a part of success.

There are hundreds of moving parts when buying or selling a home. The agent you select will need to have their finger on the pulse of most, if not all, of these activities, and there is a 0 percent chance that everything will go exactly as planned. Zero. Tom Brady didn't complete every pass, Serena Williams didn't win every match, but both are athletic legends because they overcame adversity more often than not. When they did face a challenge, got knocked down, or…gasp!…lost, they picked themselves up and went to work. I'm sure they enlisted their teammates, coaches, and trainers and worked on the nuances of their game and technique. They learned from their failures and improved, and the same can be said from the best Realtors in the business.

Conflict exists everywhere. When there are many parties involved in a process or event, communication and expectations can become strained. Find the agent who has the best communication plan and provable business model in place. Have them show you what checks and balances they have created for a variety of challenges, from home and client safety to negotiations gone awry. Everyone is smiling when the sky is blue, the sun is shining, and challenges are minimal or nonexistent. How does your agent react when the first cloud rolls in? Managing expectations is the single most important aspect to maintaining a healthy and rewarding relationship with clients. Reputation is so important in this business, and working through challenges or sticking points is what solidifies a good reputation. There are always options, always choices. Through my past and present businesses and many interpersonal interactions, I have learned a lot about managing the expectations of some pretty important people. Imagine telling a celebrity home seller that no one showed up for a heavily marketed open house. Needless to say, that doesn't have to happen if we have a great structure in place for managing anticipations. Here are the five recommended things great agents do to manage your expectations.

1. **Be Honest from the Get-Go.** Though it may sound impossible, I always tell potential buyers and sellers in the very first conversation that there are no guarantees. We have quantifiable results and campaigns and implementation. But as with most things in life, there are too many factors at play to make any grandiose promises. I can't predict whether a buyer will like a home or a seller will accept a lower offer than asking price. Although it may feel uncomfortable, I think that saying this clearly and in no uncertain terms positions you to take a leap of faith in our work and also helps you to understand the process behind it. The best agents will always tell you the truth, even if it is not what you want to hear.

2. **Under-Promise, Over-Deliver.** This old adage is one to live by. Great agents promise clients that they will have immediate and constant access to them and their team; that they will work on their behalf every day; and that if nothing else, it is guaranteed that they will have progressive, trackable steps to success. After that, when offers start to be presented, it's much more appreciated!

3. **Anticipate Client's Needs before *They* Know Their Own Need.** This definitely takes time and practice, but in truth, no one knows our business as well as we agents do. We know when things are going great or when we need to ramp up our efforts. It's so important to utilize our skillset to anticipate wantrs and needs, and be ready for the next steps and upcoming chanllenges we foresee. An ounce of prevention is worth a pound of cure.

4. **Constant Communication.** As agents, we are in the service business. We just happen to help you buy and sell homes. That means being bubbly, bright, and (almost) always available. While of course it's important to set boundaries so that we can all maintain a rewarding personal life, it's critical that clients know they can gain access to us as needed. Set times and standards for review, update,

and simple check ins keep everyone congruent. Progress reports show a clear delineation of the work that was done over the course of a week or month. A simple e-mail detailing tasks completed for the week shows you what you're paying for, and keeps us all with an eye on the prize.

By following these and similar steps, great agents will build stronger, more communicative relationships, and most likely achieve better results for you, too.

The Last Word: Don't concentrate on mistakes; concentrate on response and results. Outcomes can be made positive if the work ethic, integrity, and process are in place.

CHAPTER 11

Boy Scout's Motto

"The secret to life is honesty and fair dealing. If you can fake that, you've got it made."
—Groucho Marx

I ntegrity is a difference maker in all facets of life. People like to work and play with others they like and trust. In business, likeability, trust, and integrity are endearing and powerful characteristics, often weighing even more than the cost of a product. American Express completed a survey in 2011 and found that seven in ten Americans would be willing to spend more money with companies they believed provided excellent and ethical customer service. Here are two stories published by an anonymous author to highlight the value of integrity.

Two Stories of Integrity and Courage

STORY NUMBER ONE

Many years ago, Al Capone virtually owned Chicago. Capone wasn't famous for anything heroic. He was notorious for enmeshing the Windy City in anything from bootlegged booze and prostitution to murder.

Capone had a lawyer nicknamed "Easy Eddie." He was his lawyer for a good reason; Eddie was a skilled attorney. In fact, Eddie's talent at legal maneuvering kept Big Al out of jail for a long time.

To show his appreciation, Capone paid Eddie very well. Not only was the money big, but also, Eddie got special dividends. For instance, he and his family occupied a fenced-in mansion with live-in help and all of the conveniences of the day. The estate was so large that it filled an entire Chicago city block.

Eddie lived the high life of the Chicago Mob and gave little consideration to the atrocity that went on around him. Eddie did have one soft spot, however. He had a son he loved dearly. Eddie saw to it that his young son had clothes, cars, and a good education.

Nothing was withheld. Price was no object. And despite his involvement with organized crime, Eddie even tried to teach him right from wrong. Eddie wanted his son to be a better man than he was. Yet with all his wealth and influence, there were two things he couldn't give his son—he couldn't pass on a good name or a good example.

One day, Easy Eddie reached a difficult decision. He wanted to rectify the wrongs he had done. He decided he would go to the authorities and tell the truth about Al "Scarface" Capone, clean up his tarnished name, and offer his son some semblance of integrity.

To do this, he would have to testify against the Mob, and he knew the cost would be great.

So he testified. Within the year, Easy Eddie's life ended in a blaze of gunfire on a lonely Chicago street. But in his eyes, he had given his son the greatest gift he had to offer, at the greatest price he would ever pay.

Police removed from his pockets a rosary, a crucifix, a religious medallion, and a poem clipped from a magazine. The poem read:

The clock of life is wound but once, and no man has the power,

To tell just when the hands will stop at late or early hour.

Now is the only time you own. Live, love, toil with a will.

Place no faith in time, for the clock may soon be still.

STORY NUMBER TWO

World War II produced many heroes. One such man was Lieutenant Commander Butch O'Hare. He was a fighter pilot assigned to the aircraft carrier *Lexington* in the South Pacific. One day, his entire squadron was sent on a mission. After he was airborne, he looked at his fuel gauge and realized someone had forgotten to top off his fuel tank.

He would not have enough fuel to complete his mission and get back to his ship. His flight leader told him to return to the carrier. Reluctantly, he dropped out of formation and headed back to the fleet. As he was returning to the mother ship, he saw something that turned his blood cold; a squadron of Japanese aircraft were speeding their way toward the American fleet. The American fighters were gone on a sortie, and the fleet was all but defenseless. He couldn't reach his squadron and bring them back in time to save the fleet. Nor could he warn the fleet of the approaching danger.

There was only one thing to do. He must somehow divert them from the fleet. Laying aside all thoughts of personal safety, he dove into the formation of Japanese planes. Wing-mounted .50 caliber machine guns blazed as he charged in, attacking one surprised enemy plane and then another. Butch wove in and out of the now broken formation and fired at as many planes as possible until all his ammunition was finally spent. Undaunted, he continued the assault. He dove at the planes, trying to clip a wing or tail in hopes of damaging as many enemy planes as possible and rendering them unfit to fly. Finally, the exasperated Japanese squadron took off in another direction.

Deeply relieved, Butch O'Hare and his tattered plane limped back to the carrier. Upon arrival, he reported in and related the events surrounding his return. The film from the gun camera mounted on his plane told the tale. It showed the extent of Butch's daring attempts to protect his fleet.

He had, in fact, destroyed five enemy aircraft. This took place on February 20, 1942, and for that action, Butch became the Navy's first ace of WWII, and the first naval aviator to win the Congressional Medal of Honor. A year later, Butch was killed in aerial combat, at the age of twenty-nine.

His hometown would not allow the memory of this WWII hero to fade, and today, O'Hare Airport in Chicago is named in tribute to the courage of this great man. So the next time you find yourself at O'Hare International, give some thought to visiting Butch's memorial displaying his statue and his Medal of Honor. It's located between Terminals 1 and 2.

SO WHAT DO THESE TWO STORIES HAVE TO DO WITH EACH OTHER?

Butch O'Hare was Easy Eddie's son.

If I could teach only one value to live and work by, it would be this: Success will come and go, but integrity is forever. It means doing the right thing at all times and in all circumstances, whether or not anyone is watching. It takes having the courage to do the right thing, no matter what the consequences will be.

We live in a world where all too often often, "the end justifies the means" has become an acceptable school of thought for far too many. Salespeople over-promise, all in the name of making their quota for the month. Applicants exaggerate in job interviews because they desperately need a job. CEOs overstate projected earnings because they don't want the board of directors to replace them. Investors understate a company's value in order to negotiate a lower valuation in a deal. Customer service representatives cover up a mistake they made because they are afraid the client will leave them. Employees call in "sick" because they don't have any more paid time off, when they actually just need to get their Christmas shopping done. The list could go on and on, and in each case, the person committing the act of dishonesty told themselves they had a perfectly valid reason why the end result justified their lack of integrity.

It may seem like people can gain power quickly and easily if they are willing to cut corners and act without the constraints of morality. Dishonesty may provide instant gratification in the moment, but it will never last. There are many examples of temporary winners who won by cheating. For a number of years, Enron was cited as one of America's most innovative and daring companies. The CEO of the company knew the most important people in the country, including the president of the United States. The problem was that Enron's success was built on lies, and the "winners" who headed the company are case studies in lack of integrity.

At the most basic level, all business relationships are built on trust. This is true for both employer–employee and company–consumer relationships. To trust someone or an agency means that you feel confident in their ability to be fair and respectful, do what was promised, and act responsibly. When trust is embodied by a Realtor, clients and agents are open with each other. They are not afraid to express their true views or opinions. This type of communicative environment lets clients give their agents a certain amount of independence. In return for this independence, agents exercise increased creativity. This ultimately lets a home buyer or seller adapt to the ever-changing marketplace to stay competitive. The value of the trust others have in you is far beyond anything that can be measured, and it brings along with it limitless opportunities and endless possibilities.

Jon Huntsman Sr. is a multibillionaire who started a chemical company from scratch and grew it into a $12 billion enterprise. His book, *Winners Never Cheat*, is filled with stories taken from his own experience, in which he steadfastly refused to compromise his principles. Huntsman says that integrity is the reason he has been as successful as he has. "There are no moral shortcuts in the game of business or life," he writes. "There are, basically, three kinds of people, the unsuccessful, the temporarily successful, and those who become and remain successful. The difference is character." Leaders with integrity are not afraid to face the truth. This is called the reality principle, or seeing the world as it really is, not as you wish it to be. It is perhaps the most important principle of leadership, and it is dependent on integrity because it demands truthfulness and honesty. Many agents fail because they don't follow the reality principle.

Agents are heartily concerned with their reputation—that is, they care what the public thinks about them. This is because reputation is directly connected to business. The better an agent's reputation, the more business he or she usually draws. The worse an agent's reputation, the harder it is for the agent to gain and retain customers. Usually it is the simple stuff that derails a potentially successful real estate career, eclipses our joy in helping consumers find a home, or causes practitioners to burn out prematurely. Agents are where they are today because of decisions they have made or did not make.

So, a general word of advice to those who want to work with a trustworthy realty professional. Avoid those who lack integrity. Do not do business with them. Do not associate with them. Do not make excuses for them. Do not allow yourself to get enticed into believing that while they may be dishonest with others, they would never be dishonest with you. If someone is dishonest in any aspect of his life, you can be guaranteed he will be dishonest in many aspects of his life. You cannot dismiss even those little acts of dishonesty, such as the person who takes two newspapers from the stand when they only paid for one. After all, if a person cannot be trusted in the simplest matters of honesty, then how can they possibly be trusted to uphold lengthy and complex business contracts? A good friend and colleague of mine once said, "I'd rather talk you out of a house than talk you into one." Agents worth working with always put their clients' best interests first. No exceptions.

CHAPTER 12

What's in a Name?

"Size matters not. Look at me. Judge me by size, do you?"
—Yoda

S oon after the economy's jump off the cliff in 2007–08, I transitioned into real estate full time. Yes, the timing may have been less than ideal, but I was determined to make a go of it, and created my own brokerage, Apollo Real Estate. This juggernaut of a business completed a whopping eight home transactions before I realized that insurance, marketing, administrative work, 24/7 calls, copy machine malfunctions, and the like were NOT what I signed up for. When this lightbulb came on, I researched and interviewed with several larger brokerages before landing with a fantastic national broker in my market. Sure, I could have gutted it out through the pain of every small business owner in operations, finance, human resources, and marketing, but in reality, at the time, I "just" wanted to be a good Realtor. I chose leverage over total creative autonomy. I chose big box over self-made, which begs the question:

Does size matter?

You can stop snickering now. I am referring to *brokerage* size. We all know the story of David and Goliath...but does it apply to the brokerage your agent works for? Our industry is changing at an astonishing and unprecedented rate. Behemoths are waging battles over data; established national brands are being overhauled; and it seems like every day, some new start-up claims it will change the way real estate is sold. While no one can tell you exactly what the future will hold, we can all agree it will look different than it does today.

You know the names, even if you're only a casual observer of the real estate market. Coldwell Banker, Re/Max, Keller Williams, Sotheby's. The list goes on, and so do the ads, because national real estate brands blast away at consumers with marketing that ranges from TV spots and local signage to search engine optimization and social media. Clearly, competition is fierce for those brands. But if you're a buyer or a seller, does the brand name really matter? Here is what savvy agents, sellers, and buyers seem to care about most:

Brand Name: Brand can help solidify reputation and awareness, but if it mattered completely, there wouldn't be successful agents in multiple brands in the same market. There are multi-million dollar realtors in dozens of amrkets across many different brokerages. Cases in point: the National Association of Realtors (NAR) recently released a profile of home buyers and sellers, which included a graphic from the NAR report that showed only 3 percent of home buyers and sellers chose an agent based on the brokerage they were associated with. Brands do trigger different associations in the minds of consumers, and are typically more trusted if consumers are shopping in a new state or country and are familiar with an international name. Markets with international or national buyers will understand this more effectively. In Los Angeles, a growing percentage of clientele come from all over the world, including China, England, and Canada.

Brokerages provide tools, tips, and education, and the agent has the opportunity to use them to their success. A big box brokerage also generally has a more substantial number of signs in yards for more awareness, deeper advertising budgets, greater bargaining power, more robust administrative support, and posher office space in key locations. Recognize, too, that a large brokerage did not just appear overnight; being large is often a result of being good. From the public's perspective, it would seem that bigger brokerages should have an advantage. However, a broker can bring a horse to water, but cannot force him to drink. Brokerages and brands can provide all the tools and benefits to an agent to use with a client, but that agent could choose not to use any of them. Don't get me wrong, the brokerage matters. It's the great brokerage that does the upfront leg work in hiring the right kind of agents. It's the brokerage that makes sure their agents have what they need to ensure a great client experience. But it is the agent who delivers the personalized experience to the consumer.

My short answer to the question of brokerage importance is they matter, somewhat. The brokerage isn't the main reason home buyers and sellers work with an agent, but it is one of the main reasons for an agent's success and service offering. Certain brokerages may disagree…and they would be wrong. That's why the best brokerages are "agent centric," providing their agents with all the products and services possible to make the agent successful for the brokerage. Think of the agent as the handyman and the brokerage as the toolbelt filled with tools. The tools can't do the work without the handyman.

Exposure: Most of the branding questions or concerns, if any, would come from a home seller. Signage, overall market share, and business volume may be questions that arise from a home seller prior to selecting an agent. Sellers may care about the name on the sign, but do buyers?

It is a generally accepted fact that 90+ percent of all buyers use the Internet in some form to begin their search (or so said the NAR and Google). The search behaviors of home buyers have transformed from reading the classifieds on Sunday and then driving around to surfing an endless supply of real estate portals and home search based sites, and reading blogs to help understand the ins and outs of a neighborhood. It is common to hear a question like "Is MLS #54321 still available?" How often did an agent get asked that via e-mail in 1995, or even 2005? Which do you think agents hear more often now: "I'm standing in front of 123 Main Street, and I have a question," or, "I'm on your website looking at 123 Main Street, and I have a question?"

I personally believe that more than nine out of ten buyers use the web in their search (Is eleven out of ten a real number?), so it goes without saying that the exposure a brokerage provides online is essential for home sellers to market and home buyers to see homes. The impact of the web cannot be understated. The web, in its purest form, is the great equalizer, and those brokerages and brands that understand its leverage are benefiting greatly.

So again, does size matter in a brokerage? When anyone Googles a question about real estate, the results are not displayed according to size, company history, gross sales volume, or prettiest office space. Google displays the results according to what it deems the best page to answer the question asked. If Google feels Zillow has the best answer, then Zillow will rank first. If the local Re/Max office or the luxury west coast brokerage Teles Properties' website has the best page, then they will rank first. But if ACME Real Estate, a one-agent brokerage with a basement office, has the best page and big ad budget, well, ACME Real Estate will hold the number one position. Google cares little about many of the success metrics we Realtors held dear for years. While we have long looked at yard signs to indicate who was having success, Google looks for digital signs. Where we judge ourselves by sales volume, Google judges how the public engages with our content. And you know what? The public is becoming increasingly aware of just how important a brokerage's digital strategy is.

Who You Select: The traditional real estate brokerage has a propensity to hire anyone who walks in the door. I call it the "hire anyone with a license and can fog a mirror" brokerage model. There is such high turnover for new licensees that a brokerage's attrition rate is very high if they focus on new practitioners. One could argue that with more bodies, there is more availability to service, but the service could be suspect based on agent skill set. Large companies also generally have longer office hours, so someone with floor time is always available to answer a call about your home. With an army of agents, the company may stage an "office preview," where every agent in the office comes through and tours your home, providing more exposure. Every agent who views your home and is impressed is another agent on your sales team. Large offices often also have larger budgets and can spend more on advertising. The ad space for your particular home might not be huge, but because the broader company ad in the paper is so large, it gets a lot more attention. Again, the right agents who live and breathe the right values and provide superior customer service to their clients generally select the right brokerage for them—and their clients. This probably sounds stunningly obvious to the real estate buyer or seller out there. After all, real estate sales is a service-based business.

The Last Word: A big firm that lacks a comprehensive digital strategy will cease to be big for long. Likewise, a small niche firm that has been able to survive for decades on relationships will find these relationships increasingly under attack by the firms with powerful digital footprints. Relationships still matter, and picking the right agent who utilizes all of their brokerage's tools can be your ace in the hole.

CHAPTER 13

Personalization

*"Sometimes I pretend to be normal. But it gets boring.
So I go back to being me."*
—Ain Eineziz

There was once a traveler who was walking from a village in the mountains to a village in the valley. As he walked along, he saw a monk working in a field, so he stopped and asked, "I'm on my way to the village in the valley; can you tell me what it's like?"

The monk looked up from his labor and asked the man where he had come from.

The man responded, "I have come from the village in the mountains."

"What was that like?" the monk asked.

"Terrible!" the man exclaimed. "No one spoke my language, I had to sleep on a dirt floor in one of their houses, they fed me some sort of stew that had yak or dog or both in it, and the weather was atrocious."

"Then I think you will find the village in the valley is much the same," the monk noted.

A few hours later, another traveler passed by and said to the monk, "I am on my way to the village in the valley; can you tell what it's like?"

"Where have you come from?" inquired the monk.

"I have come from the village in the mountains."

"And what was that like?"

"It was awesome!" the man replied. "No one spoke my language, so we had to communicate using our hands and facial expressions. I had to sleep on the dirt floor, which was really cool as I'd never done that before. They fed me some sort of weird stew, and I have no idea what was in it, but just to experience how the locals lived was great, and the weather was freezing cold, which meant that I really got a taste of the local conditions. It was one of the best experiences of my life."

"Then I think you'll find the village in the valley is much the same," responded the monk.

Life is 10 percent what happens to us and 90 percent how we respond.

In baking a tasty real estate cake, imagine the many types of personalities you will come across in other buyers, sellers, vendors, and agents. Preheat the oven to 400 degrees. Add two cups of buyers and sellers, and single pinches of title, escrow, and insurance. One tablespoon of mortgage or funding, and one of inspection. Add in an entire jar of house. Stir in one cup of buyer's agent and one of seller's agent. Mix for a few days, pour into cake pan, and place in the oven to bake for 30 to 60 days. Remove delicious cake and top with frosting at the closing office.

If only it were that easy. There are many ingredients that go into a successful closing, and often the agents are the head chefs in the kitchen, managing the process. For any dessert or meal, said chef-agent wants to make it perfect by delivering an amazing product and service. But a tasty cake is not the only thing that makes this amazing. It's delivering amazing *personalized* customer service that makes the experience over the top. Would the experience of this wonderfully baked cake be better if it had candles, a four-string quartet, and a handwritten, personalized note? You bet your Betty Crocker it would.

Though it is not part of the job description, the best agents don't allow the challenges of buying and selling a home to take away your joy. If done correctly, you can truly have a higher level service experience. As an example, various industries have seen such value in personalizing customer service that they've taken this concept to higher levels. I read in an issue of *USA Today* that some hotels are personalizing their guests' wake-up calls. Most hotels have a wake-up call system that will automatically phone a guest's room at the scheduled time. Upon answering, you hear a recorded message. I've always appreciated the extra effort a hotel goes to by having a live person call you and start your day off with something pleasant like, "Good morning, Mr. Brown. Thanks for staying at our hotel, and we wish you a great day." Some hotels are taking this even higher. At one stay, I answered the phone for an early wake-up call and the employee not only wished me a great day, but also offered to send up a complimentary cup of coffee to get my day started.

While traveling in Colorado, I stayed at the St. Julien Hotel, which has taken the personal touch up yet another notch. Upon check-in, the front desk team built some rapport with me. I say "team" because there were three people behind the front desk, and since I was the only guest checking in at the time, all three interacted with me. They engaged me with simple questions about any dinner reservations I might want to make, my favorite foods, and more. They also noticed that I was staying just one night; I told them my girlfriend was joining me for a long-needed getaway, and she was just parking the car. Was I ever surprised when the hotel sent up a bottle of wine, some fruit, and chocolate! The staff paid attention and picked up on a piece of knowledge that allowed them to personalize our experience. But that is not all they did. There was something else on the tray, and it absolutely blew my mind. There was a small note addressed to us both as an added thank you, handwritten. The St. Julien delivered personalized service. The staff engaged me in conversation, paid attention to what was said, and then took action. Best of all, they seemed to enjoy the experience as much as we did.

Passion is a huge part of the real estate experience. Workplace studies have shown that as much as 70 percent of those who participated described themselves as "disengaged" from their work. When it comes to home buying or selling services, agents should banish the ordinary. Most people don't consider fun a part of their daily agenda. I do. My team and I like to create a touch point after a guest buys or sells a home that says "thank you for working with us" in a memorable way. The industry is full of traditional concepts in client appreciation, from calendars and magnets to food and recipes. As you will see in our mission on the next page, we like to bring smiles to all we do, so, several years ago, we thought outside the box. We contacted a funky, locally popular T-shirt company that had unique designs and high-quality products, and had T-shirts designed that said "Agent Brown took me home." It was a fun play on words commemorating the closing we just completed together. We wrapped the T-shirt in a cool box with packaging that mirrored our brand's colors and included a personal thank you note and suggestions for how to use the T-shirt, like take photos with others, use it as a night shirt, wear it during pillow fights or arm wrestling...the options were limitless. The gift embodied a few principles we wanted to convey—we shop locally, have fun, provide genuine and personalized gratitude, and don't take ourselves too seriously. By the calls, Facebook posts, and e-mails we received with laughs and thanks from clients, we knew we had accomplished our mission.

Ralph Waldo Emerson said, "The pleasure of life is according to the man who lives it, and not according to the work or the place." As with any profession or industry, the most optimistic agents are the most successful ones. We never want to lose sight of the fact that just being is fun. Bringing fun to others can brighten all of our days, and a great agent will understand the gift of making their clients beam. External circumstances may not have the power to shift happiness or sadness, but that doesn't mean we as professionals can't assist or detract from the process.

Built on a solid foundation, a good agent will have a mission and value structure to share with you. Written or just in their business philosophy, these statements and ideas will emanate from them and personify the type of experience they want you to have. When my team created our mission and core values, we took a hard look at the things that would embody the culture we wanted for ourselves and everyone we interact with, from clients to vendors. Here is our mission:

At the Midcoast Group, we believe in thinking differently.
We challenge the status quo by providing one-of-a-kind
service that is personal, engaging, and makes people happy.
We just happen to sell homes.

Share the experience.

Taking this one step further, we developed a value system that would represent our mission and encourage us to share an experience we could express. Here are our core values:

Deliver wows through service

Create unique fun

Pursue growth and learning

Embrace and drive change

Be creative

Chase the dream, not the Money

Do more with less

Be humble

Build open and honest communication with ALL

Everybody wins

I have found that people generally love checklists. A-B-C, 1-2-3, or bullet points, people love to check off another item from the list. I am no different. I like to quantify the work I do; to create a goal that has an end so I can see when it is finished. I find that when I measure my efforts, I can track my results. In my businesses, I am constantly adding new wrinkles and tweaks into our systems to improve the overall experiences of those we interact with, from initial engagement to lifelong relationship. The accountability helps us personalize by reminding us of the promises we want to deliver on.

As we say in our mission and values, we want to bring fun and happiness through our work. One of the ways we do this is being present in the lives of our clients and vendors in a way that brings them value. Here is a short list of some of the ways we maintain this value—even prior to or post closing with us:

- Monthly print newsletter
- Monthly video blog
- Special report offerings
- Free personalized website for home search or evaluation
- Client welcome package
- Client closing "experience"
- Annual appreciation events
- Loyalty card at one-year anniversary
- Personalized connection two to three times per year
- Annual personalized market review
- Birthday wishes delivered
- Access to secret list of unlisted properties
- "$0 to a Million" investment process provided

No relationship thrives when it is one-sided. Too many professionals put their needs ahead of those they work for. The best agents genuinely want to assist their customers, prospects, and everyone they engage. Think Maslow's hierarchy of needs. Yes, at the fundamental base, you need food, shelter, and clothing, but the higher we go on our list towards enlightenment, the more we see our desire for confidence, acceptance, problem solving, and self-esteem. The more ways we as agents can find to demonstrate our willingness to help you live up to the potential you desire and also have fun along the way, the stronger our work will be.

The Last Word: Yes, this is serious. Yes, there is a lot of money involved. And yes, the decisions you make will move you toward or away from your goals. Know that you can say yes to have fun while working with your agent. You are going to be spending quality time with them in the car, house, and office, making one of the largest purchases or sales of your life; you should do that with someone you like and who cares about you and your wants and needs.

BOOK 4

An Agent's Yin and Yang:
Home Buyers and Sellers

CHAPTER 14

For Buyers

"Don't wait to buy real estate, buy real estate and wait."
—Will Rogers

In his book, *The E-Myth Revisited,* author Michael Gerber explains that there is a difference between entrepreneurs and rainmakers, and technicians who are good at delivering services, but not at generating new business. There are subtle differences in the personalities of those good at one or the other, but rarely both. Decades ago, if someone wanted to buy a home they would contact the agent on the sign in the front yard, and if interested, work with that agent to buy the home. These agents could work with both home buyers and home sellers with equal aplomb. In the mid-1980s, state licensing officials and trade organizations began questioning the integrity of representing the best interests of both home sellers and buyers. How could an agent get the best price for the seller AND the buyer? Buyers began requesting the option of equal representation. As a result, agents were required to reveal which party they were representing.

Market, finance, and business complexities often birth evolution. The best agents are specialists in representing buyers or sellers, or establishing a team with segments that do both. The skillsets between the two services have evolved. Yes, both types of representation require basic, fundamental skills that all salespeople and advisers need: the ability to manage time, follow up on leads, pre-qualify, to present and negotiate, etc. But the proficiencies of a listing agent and a buyer's agent are different from that point forward. The majority of agents do not have the total package of skills to do both, and in most cases, aren't willing to learn both kinds of skills because they are so vast. If they do, it would take years of practice, often from the school of hard knocks (think back to our 10,000 hours point earlier). One would argue Michael Jordan's basketball career was better than his baseball career, or Eddie Murphy was a better comedian than singer. You get the point. Let's break down the differences.

It may seem perfectly logical to call the agent on the yard sign while driving around your dream neighborhood searching for your next house. The sign might have a QR or text code to allow you to quickly access more information on the details of the home. This is very convenient…but beware. The helpful agent who follows up on your request for information is the listing agent, and this agent works for the seller. On its face, this is not a problem. There is no one better to know the details of the home than the agent selling it. Sellers and agents have a written contractual agreement outlining their relationship, called the listing agreement. It outlines the role of the listing agent, how they will market the property, the commission rate, and the terms of the listing. As real estate trends ebb and flow, home prices rapidly appreciate or depreciate, and properties can have bidding wars or sit online for months. The listing agent will keep the seller abreast of any concerns, but is not obligated to do so for an unrepresented buyer. As a home buyer, the key is to know the unstated facts about working directly with this representative of the seller. It is great to have someone in your corner who will represent your goals, questions, and concerns. Think of it like this: If you got into an auto accident, you would want to rely on your own insurance agent versus the other driver's.

A new breed of agent has appeared on the market over the past several years, one committed exclusively to the best interests of the buyer. Whether retained for a fee or paid a percentage of the commission, a buyer's agent can be contracted to help buyers achieve the best possible price and terms when purchasing real estate, and the upsides of working directly with a buyer's agent are high. Here is a top ten list of reasons to get your own agent when purchasing a home:

1. The agent who represents you contractually has a fiduciary (or financial) and legal responsibility to put your interests before all others.

2. This professional will assist in making you an RWA buyer—Ready, Willing, and Able—so as not to lose out on the best home for you by preparing financing, setting a game plan, and building a time line that matches your goals. Failing to plan is planning to fail. You can make a stronger offer and beat out other buyers as a result of being RWA.

3. Your buyer side agent has the ability to disclose "inside" information about the seller's position that the listing agent cannot legally divulge. If you work with an agent from the same office as the seller's agent in an unrepresented fashion, this "subagent" of the broker has all the responsibilities of the seller, not you.

4. The buyer's agent can work and negotiate for the lowest sale price, while the seller's agent legally cannot. This responsibility alone is more often than not worth the price of paying commission. And speaking of commission or fee, 99.999 percent of the time, the buyer's side, your side, is paid for by the seller and is placed inside the seller's listing agreement. It's like having the other side in court paying for your lawyer. Just like winning in the courtroom, it is awesome having the best agent in your corner in your winning real estate dealings.

5. As a buyer, you will not be under pressure to purchase any particular property, since all sales will be commissioned under the terms of the exclusivity contract. This means a buyer's agent knows they will get compensated as is listed most often by the seller. YOU pick the homes you want to see, with the characteristics you want; your agent will not need to push you to see certain homes they control or that are represented by their firm.

6. If your agent has a strong network, he or she can show you properties that are not listed in the MLS. This allows you to have a greater selection to choose from. MLS-listed properties PLUS foreclosures, bank properties, auctions, for sale by owner homes, builder close-outs, and even off-market, or "pocket" properties can be searched for, giving you added options to choose from.

7. If an inspection reveals a problem, a buyer's agent can make a crucial difference. He or she protects your interests and helps negotiate through any challenges with the property. Having been through hundreds of home inspections, your agent can share valuable experience on repair costs, negotiable items, and items of concern.

8. Legally, a buyer's agent is obligated to provide complete confidentiality of your personal motives and financial intentions. Without this confidential duty, a seller might gain a competitive bargaining edge.

9. Once you find your dream home or next investment opportunity, your buyer's agent can share neighborhood property values with you, called a comparable market analysis, or CMA. This CMA allows you to create an offer strategy that feels most comfortable to you. How much the present owners paid for the property, tax records, permit and zoning information, and neighborhood trends are all presented in a tidy report. Your agent will not feel any pressure to leave out a property that could conflict with the seller's value.

10. As mentioned earlier, once your offer on a home is accepted, all the vendors we spoke of before begin the process of getting you to the closing table. Your agent can assist you in the selection of all the services you will need, while managing and scheduling the likes of the Title Company, escrow, mortgage, appraisal, insurance, and inspection services.

Buyer Bonus #11: The best agents regularly attend outside and in-house training, continuing education, and seminars given by experts in the field so that you have the benefit of the latest and most up-to-date information related to home buying. This is a competitive advantage your professional has for your benefit versus the seller's benefit. As an example, I had a client who wanted to buy a home that had eleven offers in the first four days of it being listed for sale. The listing agent, looking for the best deal for her seller, asked for all buyers to provide their biggest and best offer within twenty-four hours. A smart buyer wants to win the bid, but doesn't want to give away the farm. The best way to do this is through experience and education. To combat this concern, I suggested to my client that we use an escalation clause, a little-known negotiation tool that allows a buyer to set a price and "escalate" that price by a number up to a certain cap. When presented to a seller or seller's agent, it can look like this:

"Buyer offers $2,000,000 and will increase price to beat the highest offer by $20,000 up to $2,100,000."

By using this clause, my client won the bid and didn't leave more money on the table than he had or wanted to. He would not have won if we had not used this concept, and I would not have offered it if I did not have the education and training to use it.

So much can happen when making a purchase, and having representation gives you peace of mind that all challenges and concerns will be addressed. Picture this, buying a home is like taking an airline flight across the country. When you start on your trip, you have no idea how the trip will go. In this example, neither do the pilots. You could run into turbulence, or you could have a smooth flight and land on time. Certainly, the pilots will try to use their experience to navigate around the storms and go for the smoothest flight plan, but if they're honest, they can't promise a turbulence-free trip. Their job is to get you to your destination in the least time and with the least aggravation, while keeping you informed throughout the trip. Same goes for your buyer's agent.

The Last Word: Understand the different types of agents at your disposal, and find the one with the skill sets that are best for you and your goals. As a home buyer bonus, turn to the Free Gifts section at the back of this book to get a copy of our guide, "Eighty-eight Points of Home Buyer Turbulence and How to Avoid Them."

CHAPTER 15

For Sellers

*"In selling, as in medicine, prescription
before diagnosis is malpractice."*

—Tony Allasandra

Picture a three-legged stool. Wooden, sturdy, and short, each leg is just as important as another for the stool to stand. One is no longer than the others. None are loose, cracked, or broken. The success of the stool depends on the three legs each carrying their own weight.

The same can be said about selling a home. There are three pillars, or stool legs, of a successful home sale. The legs are called product, promotion, and price. As long as each leg is solid, the stool stands, and the home sells. If one leg is wobbly, the stool topples over, and the home does not sell. This might be a simple analogy, but it is a 100 percent accurate one. As a home seller, it is rare that we get into the mind of the ideal home buyer. In reality, this is one of the first things we should do. How do we position the home to sell? Once prepared, what are our best promotion and marketing efforts? What price will bring me the most offers and meet my goals? Selling in "as is" condition, with a cheap marketing plan and a high price, will get you nowhere. Generally, the keys to a top-priced sale are having a product that is better than the competition, at a fair price, and that is exposed well to the right type of home buyer. The marketplace will take care of the rest, and generally, the quicker the better. The longer a home sits, the more tired it gets and the lower the price goes. Again, basic supply and demand. Let's look at how the best agents make sure the stool has the strongest legs possible by examining each of them.

Product: As Tess Flanders said, "Use a picture; it's worth 1,000 words." Though home is where the heart is, it is still a product that your future buyer will want to make their own. As a seller, it's time to start thinking of your home as a product to be sold on the market. Once for sale, your home becomes less about where you live or where you've made memories and had life experiences, and more about what will make a buyer bring an offer. To achieve top dollar, you have to look at your property through the eyes of prospective buyers who will be touring your home. You have to focus on what buyers are looking for.

Before you are actively selling on the market, great agents will help you think of your home as a product on the shelf at your home goods or grocery store. Buyers walking up and down those aisles looking at their options aren't any different from buyers walking through open houses. Remember, over 90 percent of buyers are looking at hundreds of homes and photos online. Like any product for sale, you want your home to stand out and be as appealing as possible. Start by having your agent review your home and offer suggestions and ideas for the best positioning. Great agents will offer to bring in a professional home staging or design company as an added set of well-trained and arbitrary eyes to discuss constructive changes to your home, ways to make it more appealing, and ways to show it exceptionally well to help it yield the greatest possible price from an interested buyer. Often, any potential changes will include depersonalizing the home, decluttering, and doing any improvements that will help show the home well to the ideal buyer prospects. You want buyers to walk through your home and imagine themselves living there. You don't want them thinking they're walking through someone else's home. Simple things such as taking down photos, personal or religious items, and diplomas are a good first step.

For those homeowners who've spent a lifetime in their home, a lot of emotions are attached to it. It could be where you brought home your firstborn or where you were living during some major life changes. Deciding to sell the home you love can bring up all kinds of emotional or psychological conflicts. It can be these acts of clearing out the clutter, removing some furniture, and/or making small improvements to the home that tugs at the heart. Repainting your favorite man cave or craft room to a more neutral color, taking down and packing up your family photos, or transforming your comfortable living room into more of a staged look can create incredible stress. Awareness is key. Know that it's normal and highly likely that you'll experience strong feelings about selling your home. This is all part of the process of changing your lifestyle. A great agent can help you keep in mind the reason for your move and the goals that you have, as they will serve as your guiding light.

Remember too, that though your home is different, unique, and special, a new buyer will not see all the experiences you have had and why you think it is wonderful. They want to formulate that opinion themselves. As a seller, it is easy to feel your home is the only one in the world with upgraded landscaping, a new set of lights, or anything else that makes your home worth tens or hundreds of thousands of dollars more than the home across the street that sold for less. If I was given a dollar for every home seller I know who thought their home was one of a kind and totally incomparable, well, I'd have a lot of dollars. Buyers do not see the same value in your koi pond or shag carpet as you do. You have to review the pros and cons of your home, and if you want to maximize return (i.e., price), you need to maximize the product to match what will bring this higher price. Upgrades rarely pay for themselves, but there are two spaces that can make or break a home sale: the kitchen and master bath. From minor edits to major overhauls, the best agents will guide you through a cost benefit breakdown, showing you what return you can expect from your efforts. This will give you the summary you need to decide your threshold of cost and time versus return.

Smart sellers understand they're selling their homes and also making a financial decision. Smart agents will help highlight this well in advance, allowing you to slowly start to emotionally detach from the home and start thinking of the financial decision and transaction that's about to take place. In reality, none of the upgrades have to be done. Homes sell every day and in every condition. If I had the worst rundown condo selling in Chicago near Michigan Ave. for $1, I would find a buyer in less than five minutes. You do not need to gut your kitchen and build it to look like it was made for Wolfgang Puck. Just know the more you do, the more value you receive. You will appraise for higher, sell faster, and receive a higher price. Many sellers believe it makes more sense to leave a big project for a home buyer to do themselves in the way they want, but there aren't many buyers who want to pay top dollar for a home with paneled walls or autumn gold appliances. These sellers are appealing to the wrong type of buyer if they want a decent price. That buyer wants a deal, and is going to present lower offers because they will have to spend money to improve the home to compare to the renovated beauty they saw online a few hours ago. For most buyers, they will have to take the time to find vendors, do repairs, buy materials, and work with a contractor to make the home just right.

For some sellers, timing and effort is more important than top price. However, if you want to maximize return, you will want to make your home as show ready as possible. My clients have renovated or built hundreds of homes for resale and profit, giving me a keen eye for finding value while mitigating cost. A great agent can help you do this as well, without breaking the bank.

Promotion: It's astonishing how some agents have the worst judgment in marketing a home or property. If you've never heard of www.badmlsphotos.com and you are looking for a good laugh, you need to visit. The site is built around what some real estate agents think is acceptable in one of the major pillars in marketing, the photography. Some of the pictures are almost too ridiculous to be true, but this kind of poor home marketing goes on daily. Bad home descriptions, poor home preparation, and misrepresentation of home details are commonplace.

A homeowner or agent could spend gobs of money trying to cross-pollinate broad market areas, but doing so is the same as casting a fishing net over and over again into an opaque sea. Without a target, that tremendous effort is almost entirely wasted, and you are spending money with a minimal chance to recoup your investment of time and effort. However, if you choose the right lure and focus on the places where you know your prospects are, then your efforts are going to pay off. A professional Realtor takes the time to craft something that will entice a buyer to want to visit your house, while the exceptional one creates an all-encompassing lifestyle plan, one that will systematically and deliberately position your home as one of a kind. The goal is to make the home a magnet that attracts ideal prospects immediately.

To create an effective marketing plan, you must realize that each home is a snowflake, unique in many ways. Location, price, current market trends, bedrooms, bathrooms, square footage, amenities—there are numerous variables to highlight in making up a successful plan to market a home. However, there is a template of best tools to use. Though the following text only scratches the surface of all the details that go into an effective marketing campaign, it at least gives you an idea about what is involved in providing the best opportunity for home selling success. Now that we've skimmed the surface of what not to do, it's time to see the pillars of a strong marketing outline.

Interconnectivity of Message: People are inundated with advertising nearly everywhere they turn. Whether scanning the ketchup label as we squeeze out a dollop, or driving down a highway passing dozens of billboards, we are affected by many forms of marketing. Selling a home is no different. Marketing professionals are familiar with the rule of seven—the idea that it takes a consumer at least seven times seeing a product or company advertising before he or she feels compelled to make a decision—and they leverage it. Through tracking technology, I have seen prospective home buyers look at a single home online dozens of times before calling me about it. The challenge for a good agent, then, is to slide the marketing and advertising into the consumer's awareness without being irritating or simply ignored. The goal of cross-media marketing is to place a home continually front-of-mind, sharing it with consumers in a variety of mediums. If done correctly, the market match will connect with the right buyer. Remember, it only takes one closed buyer to make a happy seller.

Lifestyle Analysis: Now is probably a good time to expose a myth in the real estate industry, as it will guide us to a better understanding of correct home marketing and best practice advertising. That myth is this: Most real estate pros around the world believe they are selling houses. Many real estate ads only seem to prove that practitioners can count—"four bedrooms, three bathrooms, and 3,200 square feet." It is vitally important to understand that you are not selling a house. What you are selling is…drum roll…the experience of living there.

When a buyer purchases a home, they are not just buying a house; they are buying a *lifestyle*. If you think of any product, from Rolls Royce to Versace, there is a cheaper, more cost-effective alternative.

Many could own a Honda Civic or a Walmart handbag that provides the same utility...so why would someone pay $300,000 for a car or $30,000 for a purse? Because certain consumers relate to these products. The car, bag, or widget makes them feel the way they want to feel. This is lifestyle choice over economic choice. Homes are the same way; they are unique, offering a variety of amenities and signature wonders that others do not have. When you have a unique product, the job of the marketer is to find the target market that is an EXACT match for this product. A wine aficionado may want a wine cellar in their home, a car collector would like a heated eight-car garage, and so on. The key is to create a message to match the market. To initialize a lifestyle marketing plan, experienced agents will note in detail all the features and benefits of the home, grounds, neighborhood and community, including amenities, home characteristics, utility billing information, legal ownership, and property history. Once an initial prognosis is developed, the marketing machine can be turned on full-steam ahead. This blitz could look something like this, with every aspect of the plan having measurable success rates:

Professional Copy: There is a picture that prospective buyers have in their minds: living in their new home, which may have an extra bedroom or two so the kids can have their own space and privacy, and the resultant family harmony. Or perhaps the extra entertaining areas, where owners can host their friends in various styles or ways. The first thing to remember is that home buyers care about themselves more than the home seller. We can't blame them, but this is a key point. We are selling to THEM, and they want to feel like the ad was written solely for their eyes. Good copy should make them feel like you understand their goals and dreams better than they do. Real estate copywriting is all about the other person. Here is how we can pique their interest:

- Focus on how they will feel when they see this home or live in it,

- Bring up how they will benefit from the purchase, and
- Explore how this will lessen their pain points.

Once an ad matches the picture the prospective buyers have in their minds about what it will be like living there, you have a match and have now attracted the right buyer. We can now place this copy in all of our mediums to cast the widest targeted net.

Pictorial: There is a major facet of real estate sales that's the most often undervalued, and that is the presentation of the actual product, the home. If you want to improve your odds of selling your home sooner, and for top dollar, the proper presentation starts with artistic level, story worthy photography done by a truly professional real estate photographer. Colors and contrasts, light, the placement of the sun in the sky, the time of day, and so many contributing factors play a role in the types of successful images that enhance a home. There's a measurable difference between a pretty home picture and one that GRABS your attention and portrays the warmth of the inner and outer spaces as the new owner of that property. If you need a refresher of what not to do, go back to www.badmlsphotos.com.

Online Tools: No matter the product or service, today's consumers want accurate information quickly and conveniently. With so many buyers searching the web, real estate professionals must harness the features and capabilities of online marketing to meet these ever-increasing needs. The MLS is a powerful tool, but it cannot cut it by itself. Website syndication, video, virtual tours, blogging, social media, individual property websites, and mobile capabilities are just a few of the concepts put in play in the best web marketing campaigns.

Signage: The yard sign can be one of the most effective advertising weapons in your arsenal. Drive-by traffic and word of mouth are powerful tools, and having a great looking sign that attracts attention and stands out from the crowd is a winner. The best signage today cross-pollinates with your online presence, giving instant access to property information while tracking hits, or contacts that connect from the yard signs, text message sign riders, and lead tracking technology. Follow these tips to get the most out of your real estate signs in today's evolving marketplace.

Print: In some countries—particularly the United States—real estate advertising in newspapers has diminished dramatically, while in countries such as Australia and New Zealand, print advertising continues to thrive. Since we need to see the same ad or message several times before we'll respond, having another medium can only help. Be it newspapers, brochures, magazines, flyers, or all of your selected media, once you've created a great ad, repetition and consistency of the message are key. Put the message in front of your buyer audience multiple times over multiple channels to get the best results. The best print opportunities to use are:

- Seller's disclosures that highlight material facts about the home.
- A custom home marketing book to be placed in the home for buyers and their agents to reference. Not all agents will be as knowledgeable about your home and the neighborhood. This guide is left in your house and will answer most buyer questions about your home, the community facilities, schools, and the surrounding area, as well as home features, area map, plat/lot map, floor plan (if available), tax information, and other possible buyer benefits.
- In-home brochures, which are "mini me" versions of the home book for the buyers to take with them.
- Mail style brochures and/or postcards to be sent by postal, pony express, or carrier pigeon; any way to get the word out.
- Newspaper and magazine advertising. Generally, I use this sparingly, and only to drive traffic. Placing large banner

style advertising with no call to action or market match is like throwing a dart at a map to decide where you want to travel. You'll go somewhere, but there's no guarantee of having the trip you want.

These tools present wonderful opportunities to leave a lasting impression. Content, story format, size, color, and design are critical for print material to have any value. There should be movement between the text, photos, and any other design elements so that the viewer's eyes move around the page.

In-Home: If you've attended a museum or art gallery tour, you have experienced the power of a personal presentation from the tour guide as he or she shares stories, anecdotes, and history related to the tour. People have a tendency to learn and process information differently. Approximately 65 percent of the population learns visually, 30 percent tends to retain information after hearing it, and about 5 percent of the population picks things up through touch or imitation. Knowing this, a mixture of marketing styles can be used to accentuate and present your home to the largest pool of buyers. Open houses, broker opens, and events in the home are excellent ways to tap into the 40 percent of home buyers who will want to hear about or feel the home. In addition to creating further interest in your property, this can increase the number of agents who would come to preview or show your home.

Prelist: The Secret Sauce: A friend's grandmother had a special gravy she used to make. No one in my friend's family knew the recipe, but they were always trying to get the ingredient list because it was so tasty and they wanted to make it on their own. Many had ideas as to what was in it, but never knew the amounts or exact ingredients; attempts to replicate were adequate at best, inedible at worst. Grandma always joked she wanted to hit seventy before she imparted the secret (she did, at her seventieth birthday), and as a running family joke, the grandkids tried many creative ways to get ahold of the ingredients list, to no avail.

Like Grandma's secret gravy recipe, home buyers want to know about secrets. This might be a home not yet on the market that matches their goals and dreams. It might be a steal of a deal they can't pass up. Selling a home can utilize these secrets to the advantage of the sale: build demand, get multiple parties interested, and create a bidding frenzy. The format for doing this is to create a secret, a deal that others want. Our team built, tweaked, tested, edited, and engineered a prelisting plan that has shown massive success in selling a home. It is such a strong format, so positive in results, that we only roll it out for the most dedicated of home sellers who are willing to have their home 100 percent ready for sale. Intensive, but near perfect in its desired result. Some of the ingredients for this secret sauce include:

- A "100 percent sale ready" home guarantee
- Sales copy marketing that sings to the right home buyers
- Needle in a haystack buyer mailing, directed at targeted buyer matches
- Marketing the secret home to secret online RWA buyers
- VIP professional and personal referral network
- Reverse prospecting plan to the right agents
- Community guerilla marketing
- Sneak peek and red carpet event(s)

These components make up portions of the program, but not the preparation. I'd love to share with you all the ingredients of the secret sauce, but this story would get to be too long. If interested in learning more about this technique, go to the Free Gifts section at the back of this book.

Price: The often, quite literally million dollar question when it comes to real estate is: How do you sell your home for the most money? It may go without saying, but what you could get yesterday you might not get today. The list of potential pricing factors is long, including conditions and market trends. However, one of the largest pricing determinants is the realtor you choose. They could literally make or break your sale. Yes, if you list your home for a dollar, pound, yen, or loonie, it is going to sell, no matter the marketing plan. As long as the house isn't built on a toxic waste dump, or similar detriment, it would sell at that price.

Since most sane people want more than a dollar for their home, understanding the process of pricing is critical for a successful sale. All too often, homeowners believe an agent's primary role is to determine the value of their home. In reality, agents must develop a pricing strategy based on market data and the conditional factors the homeowner controls. There is no exact price for real estate. The market determines value. Ultimately, the burden of pricing is on you, the homeowner, but with an assist from your realty professional.

If you are a homeowner, think back to when YOU were buying a home. Remember when a great deal came on the market and everybody was swarming to the open house? Your agent wrote your offer on the hood of her car outside the home, only to find out there were ten other offers and they were going above the asking price. This "bargain price" created an auction effect and got people excited. This is how banks are pricing their homes as well. If you want your home to move quickly and for the most amount of money, this can be an effective, winning strategy. So why don't sellers do it more often? It's because there's a little voice inside of our heads (and wallets) that says "what if." "What if" I can get $50K over market value? "What if" I don't get multiple offers, and I only get one offer? Often, fear and greed hold us back from making smart choices. Don't feel bad though, even real estate agents are guilty of senselessly overpricing their homes. Somehow, when it's our turn to sell, all of our market knowledge can get thrown out the window as we too chase the almighty dollar. Even though we know that if someone were excited enough about our home to pay $50K over appraised value, their lender won't loan the money if the value isn't there. No loan, no buyer. Even though we know the market drives pricing, and one offer means we may still be overpriced, we can still have little voices telling us ours is different. It's human nature. The bottom line is, almost always, an overpriced house will sit on the market longer and sell for less than it should have had it been priced strategically from the beginning.

For most sellers, we want the highest price we can get more often than not. With this as the only variable, it is easy to ask ourselves why we wouldn't try to find an agent that can promise to sell our home for the highest price. But there is a problem with a best price agent; they still have to get you that price. It is one thing to offer it, another entirely to get a buyer to close on it. If you say you want to go with the highest price, you could end up overpricing your home by the greatest amount with an agent whom you believe to be the least competent to attain it. Would you list with an agent who promised you perfect weather during the listing period? Of course not, because you know an agent can't control the weather. We have as much control over the weather as we do over the value of your home. We can't make this promise. Promises don't sell homes, processes do.

Yes, there is a definitive process for establishing a home price. Once proven, it is as simple as a basic math equation. $A + B = C$. To begin with, there is a relationship between cost and value. Cost is the amount you paid, plus any improvements. Price is what you ask, the amount you attempt to get. Value is what it's worth to one person, someone who needs that exact property. The problem is, that person knows she only has to pay market value. And market value is the amount that appeals to many buyers and will cause a sale within a reasonable time. The key point is that cost and market value are not related. Even if you had inherited your home at no cost to you, you would still want market value because it doesn't matter what was paid for the home.

Everyone seems to have an opinion about value and a willingness to express it. You know what they say about opinions; ask your parents if you don't know. Buyers often believe the value of a home to be lower, while sellers believe it to be higher. Many think that every home will sell sometime, but many homes expire or languish on the market for months. Expired homes are the ones that didn't sell and went off market; they represent prices above what any one buyer would agree to, often over several months. Homes that are for sale and are actively on the market often represent the current top of or above market pricing. They represent a hopeful price, for they do not receive it until they're sold. This is a bit of forecasting. Sold homes, those that had a buyer buy and a seller sell, represent actual, comparable market value. The market is the only opinion that counts. Appraisers and agents can be more objective and see the middle ground of market value, because research on the market provides factual documentation of market conditions as a way of measuring accurately. The market may not be kind, but it is never wrong.

Sellers also often want to increase or inflate value based on improvements they have done to their homes or properties. Unfortunately, it's rarely possible to recover all the value from an improvement. In most cases, very few buyers value your improvements as you do. For example, a builder sold a home for $1,000,000 that included a $20,000 well. A similar home was built next door, but the well went through harder rock and into a deeper water table, so it cost $40,000. How much is this home worth? $1,000,000, even though the builder had to spend an additional $20,000 in the cost of building it. According to the principle of substitution, value is determined not by what a seller puts IN a home, but by what a buyer gets OUT of the home—in both cases, they get water. Value is subjective in the mind of the buyer.

A common mistake that many owners make is to focus solely on their home when determining value. Yet in dynamic markets, many influencing factors are completely out of their control. We've witnessed recent dramatic market changes in which the economy, interest rates, and financial markets affected values. The simple act of a neighbor reducing a price can lower street values. A subdivision of new construction can lure buyers away from existing homes and lower their value. A new corporate employer can move into town, bringing hundreds or thousands of jobs. Market trends, amount of supply, and the like all affect value beyond location and size.

Absorption rate is a more advanced concept that can demonstrate the dynamics of market competition. In its simplest form, absorption rate says that even though a home may be "worth" more, there may not be enough buyers to buy it. If the market is absorbing inventory slowly, then an owner must price lower to produce a sale. Sellers can price higher in a higher absorption rate market, but must price lower in a lower absorption rate market.

Codependency is a behavior in which a party engaging in dysfunctional behavior stays the same while the codependent "enabler" changes their behavior to compensate. Let's say a home buyer is the dysfunctional party making a low offer on a home, and the seller overprices to compensate. The seller says, "I know the buyer will offer low, so I'm just going to raise the price so we end up at market value." By doing this, the seller ends up with an overpriced home that doesn't sell, while the buyer continues on with his or her life. Similarly, we encourage sellers to avoid becoming a pinball listing. In a pinball game, the ball bounces off bumpers (overpriced homes) to scoring positions (properly priced homes). Buyers bounce off an overpriced listing into properly priced homes instead. If your home is overpriced, it makes the other comparable homes look better and may help them sell first. A home that starts out overpriced is less likely to sell in a timely fashion, so often, motivated sellers are forced to reduce the price. It still doesn't sell, and they reduce it again. Finally, they reduce it to market value. What do you think happens? It stays on the market. Ugh. Why does this happen? Because if a home has been on the market a long time, buyers believe that something is wrong and the home may have lesser value. They think a seller may be hiding something because no one has bought it. Historical market data always confirms that the longer a home is on the market, the lower the final sale price will be. Once you list a home, the clock is ticking.

If a seller knowingly chose to overprice their home right away, they would be overpriced during the period of highest potential for buyer activity. The first two weeks is when you are freshest on the market, and the most buyers are looking. They have looked online at homes, and see yours. If they feel like the value is there, they will come. If they don't, they won't. Smart sellers will not put themselves in this position of "if." With all the items that affect pricing, what would happen if a home is priced right in the first place? Ahh, not much, just loads of buyer activity, interest, and offers. Pricing it right during the initial phase of exposure generally captures the best buyers. Did you know that up to 60 percent of sales are generated by agents from other firms? This means agents from other brokerages bring their buyers to buy your home. Overpricing will deter them from showing it to their prospects. Proper pricing improves these agents' reaction time for their clients and improves the response you as a seller get from the Internet marketing you utilize. When a home is priced right, buyers get excited and make higher offers. Like any successful process, following a proven strategy will allow you to see fact based results and information to make a wise decision. The best strategy for an agent to help establish pricing includes these steps:

1. Research homes currently on the market that buyers will be looking at in addition to your home.

2. Research homes that have recently gone under contract for sale in your area.

3. Research homes similar to your home that have recently sold.

4. Analyze the number of months of inventory in your area and your neighborhood.

5. Analyze the price and condition of the homes that were successful in selling.

6. Analyze why other homes continue to stay on the market day after day.

7. Analyze homes that expired (did not sell) and why they were not successful.

8. Consider price per square foot of your competition and Internet value estimates.

9. Call other area agents, if needed, to discuss activity on the comparable properties they have listed or recently sold in the area.

10. Obtain information that establishes value, including: What type of improvements have you done to your home in the past five years? What other features of your home make it attractive to buyers? What do you think the home is worth?

11. Get an educated overview of current market conditions, including national, your county, and your neighborhood.

12. Agent discusses with you how buyers are finding homes, how many homes they typically look at before buying, and features that are most (and least) appealing to buyers.

13. Discuss your competition and how you compare.

14. Review recently pending or sold comparable properties.

15. Discuss the concept of bracketing in order to bring the highest number of buyers to you in the shortest amount of time.

The Last Word: Like stock brokers, agents are not paid to beat the market, but instead are valued for reading it, assessing trends, and providing exceptional service. We help you stick to the overall plan. Price right and sell; price wrong and don't.

BOOK 5

Systems: The Agent's Toolbelt

CHAPTER 16
Sales Funnel

"Not following up with your prospects is the same as filling up your bathtub without first putting the stopper in the drain."
—Michelle Moore

The first automobiles were expensive and custom made; only the inventors or the rich had one. After creating his first car in the early 1900s, Henry Ford set a goal to bring the motor car to the multitudes. Ford took the first step toward this goal by creating the Model T, a simple, sturdy car that offered no factory options—just a cookie cutter, inside the box product. The Model T kept the same design until the last one rolled off the line almost twenty years after its inception.

From the start, the Model T was less expensive than most other cars, but it was still not attainable for the masses. Ford and his team looked at other industries and found four principles that would further their goal: interchangeable parts, continuous flow, division of labor, and reducing wasted effort. Using interchangeable parts meant making the individual pieces of the car the same every time. That way, any valve would fit any engine; any steering wheel would fit any chassis. Improving the machinery and tools meant adjusted machines so a low-skilled laborer could operate them, replacing the skilled craftsperson who formerly made the parts by hand. This improved work flow was a success, so that as one task was finished, another began, with minimum time spent in setup. Inspired by meat-packing houses and a grain mill conveyor belt he had seen, Ford divided the labor into multiple steps, requiring less time and effort. Over five years of testing and tuning brought forth an industrial invention—the first moving assembly line ever used for large-scale manufacturing. The manufacturing principles were adopted by countless other industries.

Business systems are not only a benefit and advantage to the best businesses, but also to the best agents, their customers, and vendors. Benefits include saved time; consistent, quality results; solutions for problems that arise; and an increased level of services offered. An agent with established systems offers you a repeatable process with guarantees and results in place that are not based on the talent, drive, or availability of one agent alone.

Have you heard the story of *The 500 Hats of Bartholomew Cubbins*? In this Dr. Seuss book, Bartholomew is ordered by the king to remove his hat as the king passes by. Bartholomew does so, but another hat mysteriously appears. When he attempts to remove this one, yet another one appears. As this continues, the hats begin to grow in extravagance and beauty. The 500th hat, covered in gold and jewels, finally leaves Bartholomew's head bare. Stunned by the beauty of the hat, the king pardons him for not removing his hat originally, and trades him 500 gold coins for the 500th hat. Wearing the hat of a Realtor is very similar to Bartholomew in that there are so many tasks to do; as one task is done, another pops up. From finding clients and managing expectations to marketing or finding properties and continuing education, the list seems endless. Many working agents work or are accessible 24/7/365 to try to stay ahead of all the work required, and it is not until the last hat is displayed that we are able to give you the jeweled hat. By delegating some of these hats within a structured system, we are able to leverage time, money, and effort to get great results, getting the hat to you faster and without hiccups.

Due to the HUGE availability of data on the world wide web, and the ease with which anyone can get feedback and reviews via social media, the relationship between agents and customers has changed. Historically, it used to be marketing that positioned and created value in a product. But with the advent of the Internet and the availability of information, the buyer now has a say in the value decision. Exact figures vary, but estimates suggest that prospects are often 60 percent of the way through their buying journey before they even speak with a sales rep or professional who could assist them. What this means is customers are more informed than ever. An agent can add value by becoming a trusted mentor who focuses on benefits instead of features, which opens a new, relational dialogue. This is important for you, as with the right funnel, tracking, and follow-up process, agents can have a growing pipeline and steady stream of home options for a buyer, and buyer prospects for a home seller. Sales funneling benefits a seller by having this pipeline of prospective home buyers at the ready, financially approved, wanting to see homes. It is a built-in target market. We are also able to follow up with home showings, open house attendees, calls prompted by signs, and home website visitors, allowing us to have a better chance of converting someone to purchase your home. This same sales funnel process benefits a home buyer by having a list of secret, unlisted homes that the buyers can access prior to selling on the open market, where competition is stiffest.

The benefit for you is in the agent's follow-up. Once a new lead comes in, contact information is collected, along with all the notes, phone calls made, and e-mails sent, and most importantly, this person's place within the agent's sales funnel. Having this information handy keeps your agent organized for you, allowing he or she to have a pool of qualified options for you even before you are looking to buy or sell. For the best marketing and buyer generation options, agents can no longer simply present the features of the service they offer. Now, the sales process used for you needs to be designed so your home or home buyer prospect knows there is value in moving to the next stage. The best sales funnels now offer buyers a free demonstration or report, allowing prospects to see real value in getting a clearer understanding of how your home will benefit them in practice.

The Last Word: By using a structured sales process and by quantifying the number of prospects at each stage, agents can predict the number of qualified buyers for a home seller, or the number of on- and off-market homes for a buyer. This allows home buyers and home sellers to have a competitive advantage in the marketplace.

CHAPTER 17

Teamwork Makes the Dream Work

"Alone we can do so little, but together we can do so much."
—Helen Keller

I magine a routine dental cleaning and exam. Prior to an appointment, you call the dental office and schedule with the receptionist. When you arrive, you are greeted warmly by the receptionist, who has you take a seat and fill out several forms on confidentiality, dental history, and contact information. When ready, the receptionist will introduce you to your dental hygienist, who guides you to one of the dental rooms and reviews with you your overall health and dental hygiene, X-ray history, and any concerns or questions. Your exam, cleaning, and notations will be completed, after which the dentist makes an appearance and speaks with you and the hygienist about your overall review. The dentist or hygienist will also ask about any health problems you have or medications you're taking and discuss how they might affect your oral health. A maintenance program will be suggested, and you will be on your way.

Over the course of this hour or two, hundreds of business practices have taken place between you, the receptionist, the hygienist, and the dentist. The experience was as pleasant as can be for this type of checkup, and was professional and courteous. However, the dentist was actively involved in only a fraction of the steps. You say you went to the dentist, but you don't really spend much time with the actual dentist. As day-to-day business goes, the dentist can't do it all. Imagine if the dentist did all of the tasks above. My guess is they wouldn't work with many clients and wouldn't have much of a life.

Unlike dentists, most agents are one-person shows with limited resources, time, and energy. They are often juggling several clients with little or no help and inadequate funding. Think back to any of the processes or services we have described thus far in this book. It is nearly impossible to give you world-class service without world-class business practices. Real estate transactions include a multitude of processes, procedures, and deadlines, and it only makes sense that it takes many skill sets to successfully complete each one. In the past, most agents promoted themselves as the ultimate "expert" who was able to fully handle each component, but let's face it, we all have our strengths and weaknesses. In today's fast-paced world, it is harder for one person to complete, let alone succeed at, all the details required to help you buy or sell effectively while providing the best service experience possible.

Today, the agents assisting the most clients weekly, monthly, and annually, year over year, work more like the dental experience above, or like Henry Ford and the assembly line described earlier. The most successful people leverage time, resources, and people to maximize their efforts. As a client, you WANT them to do this, you want them to focus on what they are best at and allow the business and systems to do the rest. If you had a heart condition, would you want your cardiologist answering the phone? Do you need Bill Gates to make, package, and deliver your Windows software? Of course not.

My first year as an agent, I held open houses, knocked on doors, and did just about anything to meet someone who would let me help them buy or sell. As my business began to grow, my phone finally began to ring consistently with prospects and referrals. This was awesome, until I quickly realized I was working nights and weekends, sleeping and exercising less, eating poorly, and not seeing friends and family—no stability. I had a real challenge: I wanted to help the influx of people who had raised their hand and said, "Erik, work with us," but not at the risk of losing quality service or quality of life. I needed to find a way to balance everything. For me, this balance would come from adding leverage to my practice.

As Mark Greene wrote in Forbes, "The real estate industry is no place for the meek and the timid; it is competitive, has high barriers to entry, and embodies the natural order of hard work and commitment delivering financial rewards. As in any industry, competition leads to innovation. In the 1990s, Realtor teams began to populate the landscape and compete with traditional individual real estate agents. As a result, today's real estate marketplace offers a choice between working with a traditional individual agent or with a Realtor team."

From the consumer's perspective, the advantages of working with a Realtor team, aside from the obvious seemingly unlimited access to an agent, is the efficiency of the team's organization moving the transaction forward. On one hand, the idea that several real estate brains are better than one, all focused on buyer and seller solutions, is to your benefit. The team can be in two or three places at one time, while buyers and sellers have ready access to someone on the team at virtually all times. With multiple agents embodying multiple brackets of expertise, clients have a wealth of industry knowledge to tap into as well. A team could have expertise and experience in beachfront, luxury, first-time home buyer, investment, and commercial properties, whereas an individual agent would be hard pressed to offer this level of diversification. With administrative staff, buyer specialists, listing (or seller) specialists, and of course the rainmaker, teams offer a broader level of service.

Teams and groups also offer smaller, less noticeable service experiences and benefits. If one agent is with a client or on vacation and there is a task or client need, others step in without missing a beat. Most active home buyers are interested in many towns or neighborhoods, and often, one teammate is more familiar with an area than another. For a seller, it can never hurt to have another person available with all the marketing and social media campaigns that the agent can offer as part of a home marketing campaign. Realtor teams offer access and a collaborative approach to the evaluation process for buyers and sellers, as well as the ability to leverage the experience and expertise of more than one real estate brain. A team can bring a competitive advantage to a buy or sell transaction by simply having more resources to tap, more people, more ideas, and more perspectives. Best of all, you pay no extra for all the added benefits. You get several agents for the price of one.

Beyond your agent's abilities and services, there are several other essential parts to a well-oiled realty team machine. First, a transaction coordinator works with title companies, lenders, and cooperating agents to make sure all documentation is compliant and in line with legal guidelines and industry standards. They are constantly mindful of deadlines and important contractual dates. Because of the many parties involved in each transaction, it's beneficial to have someone working in this capacity to ensure important details don't slip through the cracks. Second, home sellers will work with a team seller or listing agent who reviews market data and comparable properties to determine a sales price. This listing agent can offer their professional opinion and instruction to assist in getting buyers to take notice of newly listed properties. In addition to compliance issues, the best teams place a *huge* emphasis on marketing. As a third level, an aggressive marketing strategy is crucial in getting homes sold, and a team marketing administrator has the primary goal of staying current on the most effective marketing techniques and utilizing them for sales and listings. Technology is constantly improving, and this administrator is committed to staying proactive and educated in this capacity so listings are sure to receive the best possible exposure. Some of these positions may be blended or have different job titles, or descriptions, but the general concept is here.

Benjamin Franklin said that if you want something done, ask a busy person. This seems paradoxical. Why, or how is it that someone with a mile-long to-do list is usually more likely to also be able to knock off additional tasks thrown at them—whereas someone with just one or two things to get done in a day might not get around to doing *any* of them? It's because people with full lives have a good sense of exactly how long things take, how much can fit in any given day or week, and how much they've currently got on their plates. If they take something on, it's because they've thought about how long it will take, they've looked at the amount of available time, and have calculated whether it will work. Teams are no different, except instead of one busy person, you have the leverage and benefit of several.

The Last Word: Find an agent who is best suited for you, and decide for yourself if a team has the added value you deserve. Examples of value include a broad and leveraged knowledge base, experience in many challenges, structured time blocking, and being more systematic. Your time is valuable. Every consumer has a personal preference, but if the collaborative process, an all-access pass, depth of combined experience, and real estate wisdom are on your must have list, a Realtor team may be a good fit for you.

CHAPTER 18

The Service Experience

"The best way to find yourself is to lose yourself
in the service of others."
—Ghandi

A few years ago, an eighty-nine-year-old Pennsylvanian was snowed in around the holidays, and his daughter was concerned he wasn't going to have enough food to last through the inclement weather. She called multiple grocery stores trying to find someone who would deliver, to no avail. Finally, even though Trader Joe's doesn't normally deliver, the store manager said they would in this special instance. They took the order, and also suggested other items that might fit the elderly man's special low-sodium diet. After the daughter ordered around $50 worth of food to be delivered, the Trader Joe's employee told her that she didn't need to pay for it, and to have a merry Christmas. The food was delivered within thirty minutes of the phone call, and the holidays were saved for one elderly man and his family.

Excellent customer service has almost become a thing of the past. We consumers have grown accustomed to outsourced customer service departments and faceless, electronic "help." Going *above and beyond* the call of duty and providing excellent service is what differentiates a great service from an average one. You should expect this from your agent as well. Every Realtor can say that their customers are their number one priority, but stories show us that the best professionals are ready, willing, and able to go the extra mile for each and every one of their customers.

The best way to provide a consistently exceptional service experience is to structure it. Like a pyramid, the stronger the foundation, the more likely the whole structure will stand. This holds true for service, for marketing, and for all business. Think of McDonald's. You can bank on every McDonald's having a golden arch, and a Big Mac should taste the same in San Diego as it does in Boston. Like Ronald and the Hamburglar, your agent will time and again deliver the service you expect by providing a replicable model. You care about your professional's ability to help you find the right house or sell your existing home, all while negotiating skillfully and managing the paperwork. Systems work to make this happen, as structure provides the outline of experience. To highlight, let's look at a small sampling of the steps a realtor takes from a buyer's offer to closing.

1. Receive and review all offers to purchase submitted by buyers or buyers' agents to determine best negotiating position.
2. Contact buyers' agents to review buyers' qualifications and discuss offers.
3. Evaluate offer(s) and prepare a "net sheet" on each for comparison purposes.
4. Counsel the client on offers. Explain the merits and weaknesses of each component of each offer.
5. E-mail or deliver seller's disclosure form to buyer's agent or buyer (upon request and prior to offer being made, if possible).
6. Obtain prequalification letter on buyer from loan officer. Confirm buyer is prequalified by reviewing prequalification letter and calling loan officer, if possible.

7. Negotiate highest price and best terms for client and their situation.

8. Prepare and convey any counteroffers, acceptance, or amendments to buyer's agent.

9. When an offer to purchase contract is accepted and signed, deliver signed offer to buyer's agent.

10. E-mail or hand deliver copies of the contract and all addendums to the closing title company.

11. Verify earnest money is promptly submitted to the escrow agent.

12. Deliver copies of fully signed offer to purchase contract to client.

13. E-mail/deliver copies of offer to purchase contract to selling agent.

14. E-mail/deliver copies of offer to purchase contract to lender.

15. Provide copies of signed offer to title agency.

16. Advise client on handling any additional offers to purchase that may be submitted between contract and closing.

17. Change status in MLS to under contract.

18. Coordinate home inspection and handle contingencies, if any.

19. Contact lender weekly to ensure processing is on track. Relay final approval of buyer's loan application to client.

20. Review home inspector's report.

21. Assist seller in identifying and negotiating with trustworthy contractors to perform any required repairs.

22. Schedule appraisal.

23. Provide comparable sales used in market pricing to appraiser.

24. Follow up on appraisal.

25. Coordinate closing process with buyer's agent and lender.

26. Update closing forms and files.

27. Ensure all parties have all forms and information needed to close the sale, and confirm closing date and time.
28. Assist in solving any title problems (boundary disputes, easements, etc.).
29. Work with buyer's agent in scheduling and conducting buyer's final walk-through prior to closing.
30. Research all tax, Home Owner's Association (HOA), utility, and other applicable prorations.
31. Request final closing figures from closing representative at the title company.
32. Receive and carefully review closing figures on HUD statement to ensure accuracy of preparation.
33. Forward verified closing figures to buyer's agent.
34. Request copy of closing documents from closing agent.
35. Provide homeowner's warranty for availability at closing.
36. If applicable, coordinate closing with client's next purchase and resolve any timing problems.
37. Prep for or attend closing.
38. Arrange possession and transfer of home (keys, warranties, garage door openers, community pool keys, mailbox keys, information about garbage days/recycling, mail procedures, etc.).
39. Have a "no surprises" closing and present seller a net proceeds check at end. Tie up any loose ends from buyer walk-through at closing, if necessary.
40. Change MLS listing status to sold. Enter sale date and price, selling broker and agent's ID numbers, etc.
41. Answer questions about filing claims with homeowner Warranty Company if requested.
42. Attempt to clarify and resolve any conflicts about repairs if buyer is not satisfied.
43. Respond to any follow-up calls and provide any additional information required from office files.

Like the script of a play, your agent wants to structure his or her performance so you can sit back and enjoy the show. The process might seem like a few phone calls and e-mails to you, but it is close to fifty points of service being handled. The procedures are not rocket science, but merely a thoughtful progression to leave no stone unturned in the goals of a home buyer or seller.

Find an agent who has a provable delivery system and track record. With that, you will reap the rewards of a great experience. You will also have a professional ready for any problems or challenges that can arise when buying or selling a home, and one with the ability to personalize their work for you, making the experience easy, efficient, and most of all, fun. Well done is better than well said.

The Last Word: Customer service isn't about an agent walking you through the steps of buying and selling; it's about creating stories that do the talking for you. Find an agent who accentuates your story.

CHAPTER 19

Cost

"Price is only an issue in the absence of value."
—Anonymous

When you think overnight courier, what comes to mind? In the 1980s, a budding overnight delivery company set out to increase its market share over its competition by addressing value more than price. Competition between the up and comer and the industry giant was heating up, and the new company chose to express their value directly in their ad campaigns. The industry leader did not.

Looking back on their past advertisements, the contrast in styles and effectiveness between the two companies' campaigns is almost scary in the lack of success in one compared to the other. The industry leader pitched its own features and attributes and tried to set up a David and Goliath scenario that no one really cared about. The ad failed to do the one thing it really needed to do, address our needs. It isn't fun or attention grabbing to listen to a company talk about itself.

In contrast, the upstart directly addressed its clientele by talking to us about us and our needs. Their slogan, *"When it absolutely positively has to be there overnight,"* easily and succinctly expressed what

FedEx was and is. They understood what we wanted and needed in one simple sentence. Their rates were higher than Emery, the industry leader you've probably never heard of. Emery frantically pitched price while Federal Express communicated value and focused on what its clients really care about, not just what great features and attributes they think their product has.

One could argue about the benefits of low cost versus high value. Part of the answer depends on your own value system. Would you prefer to shop at the local Walmart or off Madison Avenue? Would you like your burger from McDonald's or Maestro's in Beverly Hills? How about a Honda Civic or an Aston Martin? There is a reason both low-cost and high-value options are in business. Many consumers will pay more for a product when impressed with the level of service they receive or if the business makes them feel special. We all want to feel good when we associate with a brand. Look at watches. Fashion brands like Swatch and Guess present themselves through an expression of trends and style. In their advertising, fashion watches highlight the aesthetics of the watch and its role as an accessory. For brands that cluster into the affluent market, like Omega, Rolex, or Patek Philippe, these companies tend to focus on quality craftsmanship and design to suggest exclusive status and indulgence in lavish luxury. They make us feel a certain way when we wear them.

Real estate experiences are no different. In fact, buyers and sellers often reap the benefits of an agent with a higher fee. What? Read that last sentence again. The more expensive practitioner in any field generally offers a more personalized approach, catered to their client's needs, which will increase the speed of the service, minimize errors, and provide a result that matches their client's expectations, if not exceed them. Clients who have agents who provide stellar service will reap benefits in the form of increased sales effort, improved communication and marketing materials, and bonuses of service perks...the list could go on and on. Like the quote at the beginning of the chapter, price is only an issue in the absence of value.

Think of other businesses. If you went to a low-cost auto mechanic, is it possible you may get your car back a day or two late, not have it fully repaired and have to take it back, have a dirty seat, or get charged extra for a mystery part or two? But if you went to a more expensive triple-A auto shop with hundreds of reviews and endorsements, you would probably expect a white glove experience. One could argue that the time saved, stress reduced, and service provided is well worth the extra charge. This applies to almost any industry, especially those that have a higher risk-reward ratio for you. Think big-ticket items, like retirement accounts, legal issues, or home purchases and sales. I'd rather entrust all my retirement funds to Goldman Sachs than to Jim Bob's Financial Plannin'. No offense to Jim Bob. It is one thing to shop for home goods, dine out, or travel, but a world of difference when considering a life-altering decision. It is better to put your faith in the hands of the best professional you possibly can. Buying or selling a home or property is a big investment, and can often equate to thousands or millions of dollars of gain…or loss. Homeowners have told me, "I'm going to list with the agent who has the lowest commission or just sell my home myself," or "I'm going to work directly with the listing agent to save some money when I buy," until I explain the above examples. Like anything in life, you get what you pay for.

Agents are typically compensated by commission or retainer, but I have found that commission isn't as accurate a term as "closing fee." Agents do not get paid until a seller sells or a buyer buys— sign on the dotted line, check in hand, and keys turned over. ALL of the service examples, communication, processes, and delivery of the final documents are completed prior to the agent receiving any wages. The best of the best Realtors create a service that is not dependent upon a closing or commission to keep the lights on or put gas in the car. This is critical to understand. For sellers, paying a cut-rate commission will often get you cut-rate service, like a sign in the front yard and placement in the MLS with little additional effort. Think of our previous examples of agent types in Chapter 1 if you need inspiration. Want really cost effective? There are brokerages available to list your home online for $99. What type of service do you get for under a hundred bucks when selling a home? How about when doing anything? If you said not much, barely any, or zilch, we are singing the same song.

Realize that agents and real estate companies put up their own funds to market and advertise your home or provide service to a buyer. Agents are small businesses, and the better funded and managed, the better service their clients receive. Marketing and advertising costs money—the lower the closing fee, the less incentive for an agent to put up his or her own money to market your home. A full-service agent earning a full closing fee will often drop everything to handle any challenges that come along—an agent earning a small fee does not have that same incentive. Negotiating ability is also an important skill in an agent. Ask yourself if you are willing to put your faith in an agent who can't even advocate for his or her own compensation. Think of it like this: an agent does not look at your house as a discount home, looking for a discount buyer, serviced by a discount agent. The point is that good agents who offer a higher level of service in your area will command a higher price for your home.

The buyer's agent is the same way. Since there are often two agents involved in a sale, they split the closing fee according to the listing agent's instructions. When your listing agent dropped his or her fee, did he or she also reduce the fee that will be paid to the buyer's agent? If so, you won't find as many buyer's agents willing to show the house; they'll be showing houses that offer a customary (higher paying) commission to the buyer's agent.

Let's look at a practical example of a full-service versus discount agent. For easy math, let's say you have a home that is valued at $1,000,000. Agent A is willing to list at a 4 percent closing fee, while agent B will list for 7 percent. Both agents pay out 2.7 percent for the buyer's agent fee. Let's also assume that the brokerages for both agents take the same 20 percent brokerage fee from the agent for the company. That leaves us with the following breakdown:

Agent:	Agent A	Agent B
Home Price:	$1,000,000	$1,000,000
Commission:	$40,000	$70,000
Buyer Fee:	-$27,000	-$27,000
Listing Fee:	$13,000	$53,000
Broker Fee:	-$2,600	-$10,600
Gross to Agent:	$10,400	$42,400

Of this remaining amount paid to the agent, they have to pay for all the previous marketing we listed, as well as their MLS fees, continuing education, insurance, licensure, association memberships, etc. Oh, and their time and effort, can't forget that. The numbers will change slightly based on the market, but with the average agent doing less than four transactions per year, unfortunately, there is not much margin to discount proceeds for the true professional.

Think of the service possibilities needed for a "man in the desert" approach. A man in the desert will ask for water, but also needs food, clothing, a place to sleep, and a way out of the desert. The same goes with your home decisions. I promise, you will need many things beyond the price of the service, including access to other high-quality vendors (title, inspection, mortgage, etc.), negotiation and experience in your market, advertising prowess, and everything listed previously. On such a large purchase or sale, a seasoned professional is worth every penny. I'll be the first to admit, an agent's closing fee should not be etched in stone. If we are receiving multiple transactions, if we have worked together frequently, if a customer is a recurring VIP client, if there is a speed of sale component in place, and any of the other dozens of variables that can come into play, I will entertain options that create a win–win for our clients and us. This does not necessarily mean discount, but does equate to reciprocal value for everyone involved. The best agents feel this way. Remember though, that your employer does not ask you to do a perfect job and take a pay cut at the same time.

I once heard a realty coach say that there are hagglers and there are winners in real estate. Sometimes, people really want to haggle over everything, ultimately causing them to lose their dream home or push a buyer away. Personally, I consider myself and my clients to be winners. With me, if there's something that I really want and it IS worth what someone is asking, I'm going to get it. I'm not going to get beaten out of what I REALLY want just to save a few bucks. Investor Warren Buffet uses this exact strategy in Berkshire Hathaway, and he has a pretty decent track record. One of his beliefs, and more popular quotes is, "It's far better to buy a wonderful company at a fair price than a fair company at a wonderful price." There are those who haggle and those who win. Would you consider yourself a haggler or a winner?

The Last Word: Any business, including real estate, can outdo competitors by taking one of two avenues: lowering prices, or boosting the quality and quantity of the service they provide to customers. You get what you pay for. Select wisely.

CHAPTER 20

Tools and Technology

"It's not that we use technology; we live technology."
—Godfrey Reggio

In one of my first few years as a Realtor, some of the veteran agents in our office would tell tall tales of three-ply purchase agreements, pagers, and a world without W, W, W, dot. With social media, hundreds of realty apps, and an up-to-the-minute plugged-in lifestyle today, this seems almost unbelievable. Like most businesses, technology changed real estate from the moment the first computer hummed in an office, and the change continues to this day. Just take a look at what digital content like Netflix did to Blockbuster. Tech has made everything accelerate. Everything I have, need, or want is always at my fingertips.

Empowering the consumer has been one of the main current focuses of the real estate industry. This includes providing you with more access to data that allows you to make more informed decisions while diminishing the need for less-informed real estate agents. The smarter agents embrace these technological advances and utilize them to survive, rather than continuing to stay attached to their brochures and Rolodexes. History is against embracing nostalgia as a business model, no matter the industry. As more and more Realtors are putting off retirement, it stands to reason that many real estate professionals began their careers in the pre-computer days. Home searches were conducted via MLS books that were thicker than the Yellow Pages. Obviously, that won't fly today. Agents who utilize the most powerful and efficient tools will have clients who reap the benefits of their offerings. The best agents leverage many of the following tools to the utmost to give their clients and their businesses every advantage to excel:

The Internet: No brainer here. By far the most powerful tool in real estate today. The speed with which information can be accessed by professionals and consumers alike is stratospheric, and will only continue to evolve. Online marketing is about far more than putting up an ad for your home or tapping a website for your search. It is about exposure, about getting your home in front of people. Search engines are nice for finding a home within specified parameters, but a Realtor can do more. If he or she has a high-quality website that ranks well on major search engines like Google and Bing, your home is more likely to be seen, and for buyers, the information about homes will be more detailed. Your agent can have the greatest looking website going, but if nobody can find it doing local real estate searches, then it is going to be almost useless.

I believe in home ownership. Neighborhoods without high ownership rates decline quickly, and they have very little chance of crawling back without the right support. Technology really helps buyers protect their investment by identifying areas with high owner occupancy rates. Look at any area with high crime, underperforming schools, and depressed levels of economic development, and I'll show you low owner occupancy rates. This is especially critical for prospective homeowners moving to a new area from out of the state or country. The fear of the unknown, of making bad decisions, and lack of area knowledge can be concerning, but with the right tour guide, it is much easier to navigate the ocean of information on the web. As an example, we have created a relocation checklist of websites most often used to gather information about schools, amenities, crime, traffic access and noise, tax rates, area home values and trends, and more. If you'd like this list, contact me through my info at the back of this book.

Some real estate agents realized early on that ranking well on Google would have advantages for selling homes. These Realtors began putting in the work to build a site that was respected for both its information and its listings. This is not something that can be accomplished in a day; it takes time and a lot of effort. This is no longer a new frontier on which to obtain an advantage; it is a requirement to communicate with the millennial generation of home buyers. The easiest way to find out about your agent's online prowess is to search for him or her. They should not be difficult to find. Check to see if they have reviews on sites like Facebook and Yelp.

A Real Estate Blog: There are also Realtors who have recognized and taken advantage of how powerful a real estate blog can be in enhancing their service offerings. Not only can they provide local market expertise, but an agent who possesses quite a bit of helpful real estate knowledge that buyers and sellers can utilize is able to share it this way. This blog can be audio, video, or text. Either way, it purveys important information for free for the greater good. An agent who cares enough to have a website and communicate with a broader audience, adding value to the community, is a valuable asset for you, now and in the future.

Social Media Channels: With social media having become a large part of normal day-to-day life, it makes sense to have an agent who is tied in and utilizing social channels as another means of broadcasting that your home is for sale. Since billions of people are online and on social media, this is a no brainer. Sites like Facebook, Pinterest, LinkedIn, and Twitter are visited by thousands of people daily, and a web savvy marketer will use these channels to make your home more visible to the world. A lack of effective marketing and networking, among others, is one of the many reasons agents fail. Find an agent with a good number of online "friends," "fans," and "followers." By taking performance accountability to a new level, bad performers can't hide, and good ones will stand above the crowd of agents.

Mobile Technology: Mobile tech is reshaping the industry. The Internet has been an equal accomplice in the past. Yet in the past decade, the mobile phone has disrupted and taken a few industries to the edge of obsolescence. The affected include home phone service, map books, clocks, encyclopedias, pay phones, and personal music listening devices. At one point, I had a home phone line, Garmin GPS, alarm clock, and boom box. I now have none of those items. Consumers want instant information, and the nature of the real estate business is really one of personal service. Combining these mobile websites, searches, and responses is helping agents meet the demands of the marketplace. Since there is also so much information available online, which can overwhelm a home shopper, a great agent will have both mobile and Internet-based methods to summarize important information and reeducate clients to the realities of the local market.

Online traffic is over 30 percent from mobile devices now. My desktop became practically obsolete a few years ago, as I spend more and more work time on my smartphone, tablet, and laptop. Here are some of the apps pros love to use and share:

AroundMe: Quickly identifies your geographical position and shows a complete list of businesses in the category you tap on, along with the distance from you.
Cam Scanner: Turns your business cards into contacts, now with LinkedIn integration. Easily LinkedIn profile information for your new contacts – and connect in a single click.
DocuSign: With over 50 million users, this e-mail based software allows document writers and signers to sign documents from any

device, anytime. With encryption and audit trails, this service decreases the need for paper.

Dragon Dictation: Voice recognition application that allows you to speak your notes, texts, or email messages. You can also dictate status updates to your social network.

Dropbox: Free service that lets you take all your photos, videos, and docs anywhere. Any item you save to your dropbox is accessible from any device.

Google Drive: A free service that enables you to sync, access, and share your files across computers and devices in the cloud.

Houzz: Like a Pinterest for real estate. This app allows users to find designs of interior and exterior features and rooms, connect with designers and contractors for those designs, and shop products used in the pictures.

Waze: A community-based traffic app. Plug into the driving community in your area by joining forces with other drivers to outsmart traffic, save time, and improve your daily commute and rides.

Wunderlist: Wunderlist is a cloud-based task management application. It allows users to manage their tasks from a smartphone, tablet, computer, or smartwatch. From personal experience, I can attest that it is one of the easiest ways to track getting stuff done. Whether you're planning a holiday, sharing a shopping list with a partner, or managing multiple work projects, you have access on all devices and can share tasks and lists with others.

Expansion into mobile technology is just the latest in the ever-growing real estate toolbox. It wasn't that long ago that the realty office was almost exclusively paper based, but now, reliance on the realty office is becoming less and less essential.

Marketing and Communication: Prior to online and mobile, Realtors met potential home buyers mostly through mail, referrals, open houses, signage, or cold calls. Today, agents also connect online. Like dating websites that have profiles and pictures, agents have landing pages and membership sites with search engine optimization and pay-per-click ads that drive buyer and seller prospects to them. This is not just to the agent's benefit, but also their clients. Thousands of home buyers would want to know about homes before they come on the market from my online sellers, and sellers would want a captive audience of home buyers we agents are already nurturing to send to their homes.

Virtual Reality: Online 3-D representations that let prospective buyers virtually saunter around homes are spreading like wildfire. They're constructed based on either floor plans or data collected by special cameras used by real estate agents or marketers. Virtual reality goggles, such as those produced by Samsung or Oculus Rift, can convert these representations into fully immersive experiences that make users feel as if they truly are walking through a home. House hunters will also be able to use virtual reality gear to project holograms of furniture into spaces, so they can get a feel for different layouts. Some building developers are offering up virtual reality gear for 3-D home touring in their offices. It's easy to imagine real estate brokerage offices doing the same in the future.

Even though there have been numerous advances in tools and technology, this does not mean they are perfect. I cannot think of any new technology that has adversely affected my business, but it has affected many others who have not adapted to change. Take online evaluations like Zillow and Trulia, for example. These and similar sites are filled with almost every bit of information about a home and area. I say "almost," because the diamonds are in the details that these sites miss. Algorithms cannot assess the recently renovated master bathroom or the finished basement, because they don't know that these upgrades exist. Similarly, these software programs make mathematical assumptions based on trackable numbers, like price per square foot, area sales data, and quantified statistics. If your home has a view, or if one of the homes utilized for assessment had ten dogs and smells like a canine hotel, these value determiners will not be calculated. Market pressures change from week to week and from neighborhood to neighborhood. The motivation of buyers and sellers is always a factor, as is the condition of a home and those around it. These sites cannot inform consumers of every home detail like an agent can, and have been known to be 5–10+ percent off in their assessments. On a $2,000,000 home, this could be $200,000!

There are other potential drawbacks. The costs of technology use are not necessarily dollars and cents. The problem that real estate professionals cite most frequently today is losing touch with their customers—a real struggle in a people-centered business. As one tries to utilize the many tools at our disposal to give the best experience possible for our clients, beware the agent who is a Jack or Jill of all trades, but a master of none. Technology can make it easy to forget the importance of a face-to-face get together. Our team makes it a point to offer personal contact, because e-mail, texting, and media are great connectors, but eye-to-eye contact builds relationships. We have to be careful to not lose the high-touch aspect of our business. Great agents pick up the phone and are there in person for a meeting. You can't lose sight that relocation has always been and will always be a people business. Having heard the saying, "Technology is a tool, people are the priority," the best agents embrace the importance of not losing the customer touch element in favor of the latest technology. As with any professional advancement, there will always be a curve to try to stay ahead of. The real key is not to fall behind. The best agents use the technology and still apply the proper amount of time for a quality job. By utilizing systems like the aforementioned, agents can save their clients and teammates time and money across the board.

The Last Word: As it continues to evolve and change, the real estate industry will adapt and leverage web and technology applications for your benefit. The entrepreneur who addresses real estate industry pain points will represent real change, making it easier to conduct business for you in a better way.

CHAPTER 21

Vendors

"We're all working together; that's the secret."
—Sam Walton

T wo boys, born four days apart in the 1960s, became fast friends in high school. They socialized together, studied together, even double dated. They shared a similar vision of many values, such as giving back to the community, running a business, and even making food. So, in 1977, the now young men looked into how to combine their passions. The pair took a correspondence course on ice cream making and made a $12,000 investment in their first ice cream shop, which they called Ben and Jerry's. From the beginning, they were adamant about giving back to the community, and this resonated with their customers. With over 400 employees and revenues of over $130 million per year since 1978, Ben and Jerry's partnership was a critical success in both business and ice cream.

Thelma and Louise. Batman and Robin. PB and J. There are certain partners that work better together than apart, and real estate is no different. We've mentioned the dozens of parties involved in the process of buying or selling a home. The Realtor is often asked to quarterback most of the field, making sure all the players are positioned in a symphony of efficiency and coordination. To do this, smart agents develop partnerships that will work smoothly and try to build collective business objectives. Put simply, these relationships are not just a cherry on the top of the home buyer or seller sundae. These alliances enable an agent to realize growth and service potential more quickly than when pursuing an objective alone, and they also come with many, many benefits for the agent's clients.

By developing preferred relationships with symmetrical businesses like a title company or general contractor, agents can provide vetted, professional services so you do not need to go through the time or hassle to check on references, previous work experience, and experience level. The agent will have gone through this already, and is willing to stake their reputation and customer service on the premise that the vendor partner will take care of you as they would. Your Realtor has a vested interest in holding these vendors accountable to ensure that the products and services meet everyone's expectations. Just as beneficial, if expectations are not met, your agent will work with you in resolving questions or issues. You have another set of eyes, ears, and a voice in your corner.

There can be an ethical quandary in referring businesses to others. What if the referral does something wrong? Like all relationships, business partnerships take time to develop and flourish. Agents have developed dozens of them over time, starting slow with simple goals and milestones that give both businesses a chance to focus on their strengths. They'll have put in the necessary time to learn about the other business, making sure the products, services, culture, and philosophies mirror their own.

With the development of these relationships, the agent and their vendors improve communication, work flow, and cost structure, all while creating best practices that improve the end product for you. With all the moving pieces that happen in a typical home purchase or sale, strong business relationships and understanding will provide a better early warning system of risks as well. By embedding in the transactional communication chain of home buying or selling and improving the flow of information, business partners ensure that the relationship is able to respond effectively when the unexpected happens. We are never going to get the same degree of control over our external suppliers as we do over the internal network, but reputable agents have processes in place to try to get as close to that as we can.

Oh, but the fun does not stop there. By working together, agents and their business relationships can combine communication and marketing streams, and consolidate purchases to leverage volume. The discounts they create internally can pay for extra or higher quality services for clients. Again, a win–win. These cost savings or improvements also give agents and vendors the opportunity to innovate within their business relationships. Sometimes the best ideas and practices happen when companies look at a problem from a new perspective. By eroding organizational boundaries and bringing together teams from different areas, business partnering can act as a powerful catalyst for new ideas. Breakthroughs happen when there is a true partnership in place. They don't occur in areas of isolation; they happen when you break down organizational barriers and introduce connectivity into how work gets done.

As you can see, the partner concept is great. And any industrious agent can come up with a list of ten, twenty, even fifty partner types they would love to work with, probably in under an hour. The trick for the agent is to identify the RIGHT partners; the trick for you is to find the agent that values this. A partner with a matched vision who wants more than just a transactional relationship is a solid start. Chances are you are going to be working closely with these companies, so it's in everyone's best interest to make sure the spirit, vision, and culture are all aligned in the best interest of the home buyer or seller.

If you're still not convinced of the value your agent can bring, let me give you three brief examples of solid partnerships and how they can provide hours of stress-free home shopping and thousands of dollars in your pocket...especially versus another professional who does not have these relationships.

Example 1: Mortgage

It is typical for mortgage brokers and real estate agents to work closely together because they have a mutual goal in representing home buyers, sellers, and refinancers. Throughout the home buying process, communication is key, and a mortgage broker and real estate agent who have a good communication system and have worked well together in the past can avoid problems that arise when there's a breakdown of any kind. Having a working relationship is also advantageous for the same reason a quarterback knows a wide receiver's passing route; the agent and lender can work together more seamlessly because they know each other's next steps. Though it is unethical for an agent to "steer" or pressure you into using one of their preferred lenders, there are some benefits of choosing to go the route they may offer. For example, knowing how you will purchase a home before looking:

1. Helps you and your agent know what price ranges to look in.
2. Manages expectations of how to make offers on certain properties.
3. Lets you and them know if a special program is a best fit.
4. Keeps you from getting disheartened if you find a great home and it sells while you were preparing financially.
5. Lets sellers know you are not just window shopping, so they will give you preferential treatment for showings and availability because they know you are buyer ready.

The pros can often get you preapproved in one day, for free—and based on past experience, all t's are crossed and i's are dotted. This solid approval gives you the confidence to meet your home goals.

Example 2: Inspection
Before she moved a few years ago, a client of mine owned a home in Minnesota. Before purchasing this home, her home inspector gave her the proverbial thumbs up and reported that she had a fine house. But when she sold her home almost a decade later, her home buyer's inspector sang a very different tune than her original inspector had. This time, the inspector, who was obviously more seasoned and experienced, reported that the roofing underlayment was rotting and had been for some time. The inspector advocated for immediate replacement of the roof, showing photos as evidence. Cha-Ching! The original miss cost my disheartened client $10,000 off her sales price.

You aren't required to hire a home inspector when you're buying a house, but it's a good idea. A really good idea. As my client mentioned above became brutally aware of, inspection reports are great negotiating tools when it comes to asking the seller to make repairs. If a professional home inspector states that certain repairs need to be made, the seller is more likely to agree to make them.

Unless you're buying a new home with warranties on most equipment, it is highly recommended that you also get the RIGHT inspector. When we interviewed inspectors to find a preferred partner who would provide the exemplary level of service we wanted to see for our clients, we made sure they:

- Would walk through the home with you if requested, pointing out concerns and warning signs. Some inspectors don't want to take the time.
- Were willing to describe changing building codes and what that means for today's buyer of an older home. A house

built before 1978 could have lead based paint, but that doesn't mean the house is a hazard. The way an inspector notes this in the inspection report could needlessly scare a home buyer into thinking the home is damaged goods.

- Would provide a detailed report complete with photos and suggested remedies for problematic areas. Often an issue in a home is an easy fix, so providing details on repair goes a long way to easing stress. No house is perfect, but that doesn't mean the sky is falling.
- Would go back to the home to verify the completion of work that occurred due to inspection repair requests. We never want to assume that everything will be done as promised.

Example 3: Photography

Like anyone else with a smartphone, I can take a picture. I have the basic skills to point, click, and save. But consider this fact—most home buyers will skip right by a home that does not look appealing online. They will not read about all the great features of a home—your home—if the pictures turn them off. Clearly, lots of homeowners never check up on their Realtors after they have been hired. If there was more due diligence on a seller's part, they would often be appalled by what they see.

You never get a second chance to make a first impression. That first visual impression of a home for sale is essential to driving and maintaining interest in a property. Before you can sell a property, you have to get potential buyers visiting the property. In today's market, buyers have very high visual expectations and short attention spans, and they require clear information instantly. Prospective buyers have an abundance of resources, and before they are willing to schedule an appointment to see a property, they prefer to view the property online. The only way to entice them into looking further at a property is with professional photography.

Professional photography isn't simply using an expensive camera; you have to know how to use that camera and have skill in capturing the property at its best. Angles, lighting, and time of day play an integral part of your home's "look." A real estate photographer is a visual stager—they take the time to look at the space and take an image that showcases each room in the ideal way, even if the rooms are empty. Aerial photography has become all the rage for homes with a larger footprint, such as estates and land, allowing the entire property to be showcased in a way that didn't exist a decade ago. Homes shot by a professional average more online views, more showings, and thus more sales. Shopping for a home online is stressful; buyers are making quick judgments from brief impressions they got from looking through photos at hyperspeed. Quality real estate photography helps to get buyers to do the one essential thing you want—see the house in person.

The Last Word: No one can be good at everything. The most successful people at, well, anything, surround themselves with people who are smarter and better than them at specific tasks. Working with the right team is the difference between success and failure.

BOOK 6

Eenie, Meenie, Miney, Moe;
How to Select an Agent

CHAPTER 22

The IKEA How-To Guide

"Alone, we can't accomplish anything.
Together, we can accomplish a lot."
—James Walker

As an entrepreneur who has owned several different businesses, I would be the first person to tell you that if you work hard and continue to push forward to your goal, you can accomplish anything. In the movie, *The Edge*, Anthony Hopkins plays an intellectual billionaire who, along with two other men, survives a plane crash in the Alaskan wilderness. To make matters worse, the survivors are being instinctually hunted by a massive bear. What struck me about the film was not the trials of survival or the fight between life and death. Instead, I was both captivated and inspired by the mantra that Hopkins' billionaire was portrayed as using. Determined, contemplative, and mentally strong, the hero of the story at one point recalls a passage from a book he perused before his fateful flight. Reciting the main theme he took from the book, Hopkins internally exclaims during his fight for survival, "What one man can do, another can do." I imagined him repeating this saying over and over as the challenges he faced seemed insurmountable, and using it as a beacon of strength. By the end of the film (spoiler alert!), he is the lone survivor of the crash. Often, we inhibit ourselves. Life teaches us that if you set your mind on a goal, you can achieve it.

So after all the hubbub about the benefits of an agent in this book and beyond, there is still a percentage of people who would rather represent themselves when they buy or sell a home, or who would rather find a discounted service provider to do the bare minimum. Again, I don't necessarily disagree; you truly can accomplish anything you want. However, in the long run, based on e-v-e-r-y-t-h-i-n-g we just went over, I invite you to test your skills below and tell me you are better off making a home decision on your own or with a subpar professional versus a well qualified one.

After graduating from college, I had one of my first post school, responsible adult decisions to make: live the big life of a new car, vacations, and new wardrobe, or begin to diligently pay my school loans? Though the former was so enticing, especially since my ride was already fifteen years old and the baggy, multilayered shirt look I was rockin' on weekends was quickly falling out of fashion, I decided to go with the latter and begin an aggressive pay-off scheme to remove all school debt. My plan included living well beneath my means and buying the bare essentials, which included buying cost-effective furniture. If you have ever just moved into a new place and you were trying to do so on a shoe-string budget, you may have had a combination of inherited furniture from friends and family. Or, like me, you didn't have much at all. So you decide to go secondhand or hit the show-room at a store like IKEA, the iconic Swedish furnishings store that sells cost-effective, assemble-it-yourself furniture. Yep, this was all part of the master plan. One of the best characteristics about the assemble-it-yourself home furnishings of IKEA are the easy-to-read instructions that come with every piece of assemble-from-scratch décor. The numbers, legend, and easy-to-follow pictures make the assembly almost childlike, like Legos or Lincoln Logs. IKEA makes it easy on its customers by taking the guesswork away.

Instructions that take us from start to finish are everywhere, and make life easier and better. We use streets to get from A to B. We follow recipes to make a gourmet meal. We follow our faith's instructions as taught in the Bible, Torah, Koran, and others. Color within the lines, stay the course. Don't get me wrong, it's great to play outside the box and outside of my comfort zone. Real breakthroughs in work, science, relationships, and life come this way. My point is that there are certain areas where guidelines and instructions help us to be more efficient and meet our goals faster. There is no reason to reinvent the wheel when you don't have to.

Qualifications are important, however, finding a solid, professional agent means getting beyond the résumé and into what makes an agent effective. This entire book is filled with tips and golden nuggets of information that can help you find a lifelong adviser to assist you with all of your realty goals; it is your instruction guide. As a quick summary, use the following questions as your cheat sheet in hiring your licensed professional, and you'll be doing more than the majority of home buyers and sellers when selecting a top real estate agent.

Question 1: Why did you become a real estate agent?
Why Ask: Find their passion. Are they working for money or for you?

Question 2: What process will you use to help me with my goals?
Why Ask: Proven systems = proven success.

Question 3: What are the most common things that go wrong in a sale, and how would you handle them?

Why Ask: There are ALWAYS problems. An agent that has experienced issues and solved them will have the best opportunity to provide you with a higher level of success.

Question 4: What other professionals do you suggest we work with, and what are their credentials?
Why Ask: A team is only as strong as its weakest link.

Question 5: What do you do better than other real estate agents?
Why Ask: What is their strong point? Look beyond the canned answers.

Question 6: Can you provide me with references or testimonials from past clients?
Why Ask: Find the agent online and look for reviews and endorsements. Visit their website and social media pages.

Question 7: Why should I work with you?
Why Ask: A great question to end with. Look for the three C's in an answer: creativity, clarity, and confidence.

Once you have these answers, you can do a quick comparison based on other agents you have spoken to, experiences your friends or family may have had, or even versus your own skill sets in buying or selling. Do an honest assessment of who is going to best help you meet your goal, not who is going to be your best friend or who is related to you. Ask yourself the following questions:

1. **Who will be the best negotiator?** There are MANY people to negotiate with: home buyers or sellers, agents representing the opposite side, inspectors, appraisers, and lenders. All of these parties and more will have different views on the overall sale, and the best person who can understand, manage, and negotiate with these parties will often make or break your goal. Think of who you want in

your corner if an objection comes up from the other party, and how you would handle major or minor inspection items. Ask yourself who has the most experience dealing with contracts and other forms as well as post offer, pre closing responsibilities. Pick the person who is best prepared to negotiate price, terms, amenities, and the personal items that will or won't be included in the sale, without emotional attachment.

2. **Who will provide the best exposure?** With so many home buyers searching online, most real estate agents have an Internet strategy to promote the sale of your home. Be ready for this. The days of selling your house by just putting up a sign and advertising it in the paper are long gone. Having a strong Internet strategy is crucial. For buyers, certain markets and neighborhoods are very desirable and thus ultracompetitive. Having access to "off market" homes can be crucial to finding your dream home. Who is the best person to provide you with all possible options in Search Engine Optimization (SEO), website syndication, and broker reciprocity?

3. **Who has the best market knowledge?** Like the stock market, the housing market is constantly changing. Interest rates, politics, global economics, supply and demand, and many other variables are constantly shifting positions of strength between buyers and sellers. Who will best have their finger on the pulse of this wave? Agents connect with other realty professionals every day and trade tips and rumors, share stories, visit homes, and hear who sold what and for how much above or below asking price—in real time. Their views are professionally honed and not personal, allowing them to be impartial about what they see every day in the market. Pick the best person who can

objectively review home and market characteristics for a home buyer or seller.

4. **Who has the time?** I won't belabor this point, but this entire book highlights the best work needed for successfully buying or selling a home. It goes without saying that this takes more than a little time and effort to excel at. To buy or sell effectively, you have to change your schedule and personal life drastically. On your own, you have to be willing to sacrifice vacations and weekends. Who is best prepared for the volume of calls one might receive at all hours and the appointments that might or might not materialize? Will you be able to leave home, knowing you may miss the perfect buyer? Do you have job conflicts and aren't always available? The ability to create a solid foundation and make any necessary midgame adjustments is key to your success.

5. **Who will net or save you the most money the fastest?** Many homeowners or buyers believe that they will save the real estate commission by working on their own. Not so fast. Depending on your market area, the National Association of Realtors states that home sellers make 15–25 percent more money by using the right agent than by selling on their own. The best do the paperwork correctly the first time, prep the home for sale, help buyers with financing, minimize the time it takes to buy or sell, and have enough time and experience to field any question or concern as they arise. Factor in the time, money, and trial and error effort to see if the best agents pay for themselves.

The Last Word: Before you decide to take on the challenges of selling or buying your house on your own instead of selecting an agent, ask the right questions and do the right research. Make sure you don't miss the diamond in the pile of coal. Here are five big reasons why you may want to work with the best agent money can buy:

1) They will increase your wealth.
2) They will reduce your stress and save you time.
3) They protect your best interests and avoid pitfalls.
4) They provide marketing based on proven systems and experience.
5) Their reputation opens doors to other buyers or sellers.

CHAPTER 23

The Big Why

"We are what we repeatedly do. Excellence, then,
is not an act, but a habit."

—Aristotle

What now? That noise you hear, my friend, is the sound of applause from the author. For one, congratulations. You are as smart, if not smarter, than the majority of real estate agents currently in the business. By knowing the details of a successful agent experience, you now know what it takes to find the right professional to assist you with not only achieving your goals, but exceeding them. Extraordinary results are yours to experience.

I have often been asked why I do what I do. Why I chose this path over the joys of being an astronaut, a lawyer, or a basketball player. Simply, I believe in what a home represents. I don't mean four walls and a roof over our heads. I think Dorothy was spot on; there's no place like it. As we journey through life dodging the occasional wicked witch, it's comforting to know that a familiar door, a comfortable bed, and perhaps even a munchkin or two await just across the threshold. I have read and heard what many have to say about hearth and home, and wanted to provide just a small sampling from across the globe of what people have said home is to them.

It's where I don't have to be perfect.

Home is where I prefer to start and end my every day.

A zone where my boss, pesky customers, and bad drivers are absent, and where the absurdities of the day can be shared unchecked, unedited, and without remorse.

It is a warm dog curled up by your feet at bedtime.

I can put on my PJs and sit down with a glass of bubbly right next to the dust bunnies and they're fine with it.

Home to me is my kids…no matter what happens and how bad the day can be.

Bathing suits dangling from the deck rail, a healthy pour of crisp white wine in my glass, and the scent of the grill on my husband's shirt.

Home to me is where I am surrounded by the ones I love and call my family. It is a place of tranquility and peace.

Home is where the rags of your life are turned into quilts, lemons become lemonade, and a few extra pounds are simply welcomed as "more of you to love."

Home is where you can scratch where it really itches.

A warm bed that you can't get out of in the morning, a tiny pink toothbrush in the bathroom, and the sound of my wife's key in the door at the end of the day.

Home is my family. When the kids leave, my home will be wherever my husband is, even if it is a box under the bridge.

The characteristic that struck me most about all the quotes above was that not one of them represented a building or a physical place; each focused on a feeling. Houses get bought and sold, but a home stays with you always. Home is where the heart is. If there is one global thing we all share, no matter our race, income, religion, or beliefs, it is that we all want a place to call home.

Why do I do what I do? I love playing a small part in helping those we work with find "home." Nelson Mandela was quoted as saying, "We can change the world and make it a better place. It is in your hands to make a difference." To make a difference in people's lives by helping them find home is a gift. Service is THE reward. You have it within you to deserve the best, to find home. Pluck your own thoughts from my words and find the gold you may use to find your own definition of home. The reality is, home is where you make it…but a little help never hurts.

Free Gifts for You:
Thank you. Thank you. Thank you. A hat trick of Thank yous for taking the time to invest in this book. Now that you understand the best practices in real estate, there will be a time you or someone you know will want to put this newfound knowledge to work. Visit anytime at www.ErikRBrown.com to have my team connect you with a real estate professional who can guide you in your market. Be it Beverly Hills, California, or Beverly, Massachusetts, we can point you in the right direction.

If you would like to receive any of our FREE information on home buying, selling, or investing, e-mail your name, phone number, and address to info@themidcoastgroup.com and we can send you any of the following:

- VIP home buyer guide and top eighty-eight points of home buyer turbulence and how to avoid them
- VIP home seller guide and a prelist marketing plan to drive multiple buyers and offers
- Neighborhood knowledge web list
- Our monthly postal newsletter
- Our video blog
- From 0 to $1 million: best practices to invest in real estate

I always enjoy hearing from anyone with a story. E-mail me at info@themidcoastgroup.com

Thank you for reading. Visit us at:

Erik	www.ErikRBrown.com
Team	www.TheMidCoastGroup.com
Our Blog	www.themidcoastgroup.blogspot.com
Career Blog	www.themidcoastgroupcareers.blogspot.com
CA Search Site	www.viewhomesinlosangelesarea.com
MN Search Site	www.viewminneapolisareahomes.com

I invite you to connect with me and my team on any and all real estate goals you may have. We'd love to help you achieve your loftiest dreams.

About the Author

From humble beginnings, Erik Brown (www.ErikRBrown.com) has lived real estate for the better part of two decades. As a Gen Y, witty real estate broker who went headfirst into the housing recession and cannon balled out the other side, Brown started a home renovation practice, property management company, title insurance company, and multiple real estate teams across the country.

Brown has worked with everyone from first-time home buyers to business owners, investors, celebrities, and athletes on their paths to property success. His teams have sold hundreds of homes in multiple states, and he is a multi-award winner for his professionalism and service. Accredited as a certified luxury home specialist, certified distressed property expert, former general contractor, and overall entrepreneur, Erik has been televised as a realty news correspondent. He has been a member of Rotary International and various food pantries and local charitable organizations.

Brown commutes between Beverly Hills, California, and Minneapolis, Minnesota.